the
RATIONAL
PSYCHIC

JACK ROURKE

the
RATIONAL
PSYCHIC

A SKEPTIC'S GUIDE TO
EXTRAORDINARY PERCEPTION

sounds true
BOULDER, COLORADO

Sounds True, Inc.
Boulder, CO 80306

Published 2012
Book design by Karen Polaski
Printed in Canada

Library of Congress Cataloging-in-Publication Data

Rourke, Jack.
The rational psychic : a skeptic's guide to extraordinary
perception / by Jack Rourke.
p. cm.
Includes index.
ISBN 978-1-60407-804-6
1. Extrasensory perception. I. Title.
BF1321.R68 2012
133.8—dc23
2012007171

eBook ISBN: 978-1-60407-913-5

10 9 8 7 6 5 4 3 2 1

Dedicated to one special little lamb
and fellow black sheep everywhere

The first reason for man's inner slavery is his ignorance,
and above all, his ignorance of himself.

Without self-knowledge . . . man cannot be free,
he cannot govern himself, and he will always remain
a slave and the plaything of forces acting upon him.

This is why in all ancient teachings the first demand
at the beginning of the way to liberation was:

Know Thy Self

GEORGE GURDJIEFF

CONTENTS

FOREWORD

There are numerous reasons why mainstream science has virtually ignored and rejected psychical research since its conception in the late nineteenth century. The primary reason is that what hard evidence the study of parapsychology has produced is not reliably reproducible for the most part, and has yielded no model or scientific theory that explains how paranormal phenomena function. However, the fundamental reason for science turning a cold shoulder is that the discipline of parapsychology, often referred to as "paranormal research" by the media, tends to attract the wrong people for the wrong reasons, both as practitioners and investigators.

I have witnessed and experienced many things in my forty-two-year career as a parapsychologist. In the beginning of my career, I was a research associate at UCLA's Neuropsychiatric Institute (1969–1980) where I conducted initial protocol and methodology development for what later was referred to as "remote viewing." I also conducted extensive field investigations of poltergeists, hauntings, and apparitions. My field investigations continue to this day and exceed some 4,500 cases, one of which became the bestselling novel and motion picture, *The Entity*.

Throughout my lengthy and eventful career, I have met literally thousands of individuals working within the paranormal field. These individuals were self-professed psychics, mediums, and channelers; men and women who ranged in age from their late teens through their sixties and seventies. The one thing most, if not all, of these people had in common was a strong essence of egomania combined with intense self-righteousness and emotional instability. For these reasons and many others, I have refused to work with *any* psychics whatsoever — until now that is.

In coming to know and work with Jack Rourke over the last several years, I have been continuously impressed by his psychic gifts. In my opinion, Jack is perhaps *the* most talented psychic I have ever encountered. Jack Rourke speaks not of himself, as is the norm, but of the work and research he is a part of. While others seek to resolve personal inner-demons, Jack Rourke is a conscientious seeker of truth, knowledge, and understanding for the improvement of the human condition.

What makes Jack truly remarkable and unique in a field littered with psychobabble and insanity is his intellect and emotional grounding. Along with this, he has a healthy ego and a comprehensive knowledge regarding spirituality, clinical psychology, and the paranormal. In almost every way, Jack is my peer. In some ways I view him as a superior.

I feel honored and privileged to know and work with someone as capable as Jack. I truly believe that Jack Rourke will one day come to replace me as the ravages of time catch up with me and take their toll.

In my professional opinion, Jack Rourke is a one-in-a-billion individual. He has written an extraordinarily powerful, meaningful, and entertaining book that incorporates knowledge, wisdom, and experience from a wide variety of sources. These sources thoroughly discuss the current state of parapsychology and the rut it finds itself in due to the proliferation of misinformation espoused over the Internet and through juvenile television entertainment that is continually being passed off as real.

Trust me on this one point if nothing else, Jack Rourke knows of what he writes. *The Rational Psychic*™ is the cutting-edge of current parapsychological knowledge. If you want to know what is *really* going on "out there," *The Rational Psychic* will point you in the right direction.

This book provides the reader with a wealth of specific information, research, experience, perspective, and insight, which is rarely seen in such books, especially from a man as young as Jack. The only way you might gain access to such a broad spectrum of relevant information in this field would be to read several dozen other books, none of which would likely cover the comprehensive database from which Jack writes.

In what might have been a bleak and foreboding future for parapsychology given the current state of the field, Jack Rourke is providing a sorely needed bright light at the end of an otherwise very dark tunnel, illuminating the best path forward.

Barry E. Taff, PhD
Parapsychologist

ACKNOWLEDGMENTS

Looking back to when I first began writing *The Rational Psychic,* I realize I had absolutely no idea how much work was in store for me. In the beginning, I found tireless inspiration in my naivety. But through the many subsequent rewrites, the solitude, and the personal as well as professional sacrifices, I discovered no book is ever really a solo endeavor. As such, I have many wonderful people to thank.

First and foremost, I am indebted to the numbers lady, Glynis McCants, for her kindness, friendship, and generosity. One day, after appearing together on a television program, she looked at me and said, "You should write a book. Write a book and I will help you." True to her word, when I finished the first draft, Glynis gave a crude version of this book to her colleague Devra Jacobs of Dancing Word Group, who became my literary agent. Devra, you have been an invaluable and unwavering source of strength, encouragement, and vision. Without you and Glynis this book would not exist as it does. Special thanks to Tami Simon, Jennifer Brown, Haven Iverson, Kelly Notaras, Jennifer Holder, and all the wonderful people at Sounds True for recognizing how the demystification of psychic ability contributes to authentic spiritual growth and personal healing. To my friend Dr. Barry E. Taff: few people know that despite your medical patents, classified research for the government, and worldwide fame as a parapsychologist, your biggest genius is your heart, thank you. Thank you also to Loyd Auerbach and Dr. Andrew Nichols for your endorsements and professional contributions to the field of parapsychology. I have learned from you both. To John Holland, your kindness, candor, generosity, humanity, and passion for your work is uplifting. Thank you for being a wonderful example of what a psychic and a sensitive human being should be. The world could use many more men like you. Eddie Connor, your healing presence is a gift to the world. Your guidance as a psychic, teacher, and friend has had an immeasurable influence on my life, thank you. John J. Oliver, thank you for your friendship and commitment to excellence. Our chance meeting is a fun example of how there is no such thing as coincidence! Thank you to Dr. Caron Good for your support. And to James Van Praagh, thank you for your kindness and encouragement. I appreciate your opening a door to the mass media affording all of us who have come behind you opportunities to educate and serve those curious about psychic phenomena. Vonda Ford, thank you for your tutelage. Your early edits and encouragement helped develop me as a writer. As I continue to improve, I will always be grateful to you. I am also grateful for the professional expertise and support of my television agent Joe Rose at Abrams Artists Agency. A very special thank you also goes to all of my clients who, each in their own right, have been beautiful gifts to me. Thank you Erika Frost for your personal and professional generosity. And finally, very special love and thanks to Nicole Shepherd, Anna Cherubini, Frances MacDonald, Dino Morra, Vince and Phyllis Cecere, Mr. and Mrs. John P. Doman, Mr. and Mrs. Donal McCoy, and my Lucy. Each of you, in your own special way, has touched my heart, inspiring me to be a better man. I love you all.

INTRODUCTION

I f researchers knew exactly how ESP worked and could reliably replicate it, psychic perception would not be classified as a paranormal phenomenon.

The word *paranormal,* according to *Merriam-Webster,* means something that cannot be scientifically explained. The term *phenomenon* is defined as an observable fact or event. So when we say psychic perception is a paranormal phenomenon we are literally describing it as an event that defies scientific explanation.

In February of 2009, journalist Bootie Cosgrove-Mather wrote an article for CBS News detailing the results of a network poll on psychic phenomena. According to CBS's research, "A majority of Americans — 57 percent — say they believe in psychic phenomena such as ESP (Extra Sensory Perception), telepathy, or experiences that can't be explained by normal means."[1]

For those of us immersed in psychical research, it comes as no surprise that the majority of the population believes in psychic phenomena. The common misperception is that psychic ability is for eccentric personalities who avoid logic and indulge irrational mystical beliefs; admittedly, there is a fringe element among psychic enthusiasts. However the reality is that many normal, respectable folks — including attorneys, police officers, school teachers, white- and blue-collar professionals, and yes, even hardened skeptics — are secretly fascinated by the paranormal. As Bruce Bower points out in *Science News*:

> Surveys conducted over the last century find 10 to 15 percent
> of US and British adults report having been startled by briefly
> hearing a voice when alone or seeing something that could
> not be seen by others. About three-quarters of bereaved adults
> acknowledge having heard, seen, or otherwise sensed their
> departed partners. People everywhere, including millions of
> Americans, have waking nightmares in which they lie frozen, eyes
> wide open, tormented by hallucinations of demons or other evil
> presences that sit on their chests as breathing becomes difficult.[2]

Interest in the paranormal ebbs and flows but always seems to rebound in times of crisis. In the midst of the American Civil War, Abraham Lincoln and his wife dabbled with spirit communication after losing a child. During the Great Depression, J. B. Rhine created a parapsychology laboratory at Duke University. And since the tragedy of September 11, 2001, public demand for proof of the afterlife has motivated television networks to saturate the media with paranormally themed programming like never before.

It is not a coincidence that concerns about the afterlife — masquerading as an interest in ghosts and psychic phenomena — correspond with social calamity. In times of great distress people look to the unseen world for affirmation of personal power. However, because what "reality" TV psychics and dramatic ghost hunters teach us about our alleged metaphysical future is mostly based on the subjective — supposedly extrasensory — experiences of comparatively few individuals, intellectually discerning *rational* people want to understand how psychic phenomena can possibly be real before they incorporate paranormal ideas into their daily lives.

When it comes to the paranormal there are few things that get metaphysical enthusiasts — and disbelievers — more impassioned than the controversial subject of whether or not extrasensory perception is real. Interestingly enough, both advocates and opponents of psychic ability are often guilty of the same thing: both frequently let their emotions and philosophical beliefs influence their opinions. However, genuine psychic ability is not based on a belief system. As such you should not have to change religions, surrender logic, or adopt any exotic metaphysical beliefs to accept that extrasensory perception is real.

I consider myself a skeptic despite the fact that I have been a practicing psychic for fifteen years. I understand saying I am both a psychic and a skeptic might seem counterintuitive, so let me clarify. When I call myself a skeptic, I am defining myself as someone who questions the validity or authenticity of something purported to be fact. Keeping this in mind, we can see the probing intellect of a skeptic is essential for any reasonable conversation concerning extrasensory perception. After all, to understand the true nature of psychic phenomena, we cannot rely only on our subjective points of view, especially if they are based on outdated scientific models, religious bias, metaphysical hyperbole, or self-validating spiritual beliefs. Therefore, I see healthy skepticism as a good thing. Skepticism is only problematic when it is confused with the rigid self-serving presumptions of cynicism.

Different schools of science use different languages to talk about ghosts and psychic phenomena. A psychologist might diagnose psychosis in an individual who reports seeing or communing with spirits. A neuroscientist might explain phantom perceptions as visual artifacts of an overactive limbic system or by-products of temporal seizures.

Meanwhile, a physicist or philosopher might claim that ghosts and ESP are simply manifestations of our interconnected consciousness. Until now, there has never been a comprehensive coherent explanation for extrasensory phenomena that works across all these disciplines, satisfying both the psychically enthused and the skeptic alike.

In the following pages, the languages of psychology, physics, neuroscience, spirituality, and biology are interpreted through firsthand precognitive experiences — offering a rational explanation for what psychic ability actually is, and why it is real.

My rational explanation for why extrasensory perception is real will not require you to adopt any new age beliefs. I understand that new age explanations for ESP, involving mystical beings like spirit guides and angels, can be helpful and a great comfort. Spiritual metaphors provide emotional reassurance that those things we do not fully understand are in some way under our influence through right action or an ability to communicate with invisible beings who are responsive to our needs. More importantly, with respect to ESP, spiritual metaphors also provide a logical framework for extrasensory perception. This framework enables psychic authors to illuminate a clear and easy path to development — while avoiding the more complex causes and implications of psychic ability. Yet, if we are to truly understand psychic perception, we have to set aside metaphors like ghosts, demons, and spirit guides, which can prevent us from seeing deeper into our own mental and emotional processes. This is why you will hear me describe the inner workings of the psychic process using psychological and analytical terms, rather than the more common metaphors that carry religious and pseudo-spiritual overtones.

Some readers may not want to consider that their minds, in many cases, are behind the paranormal phenomena they are curious about. Admittedly, it is easier (and perhaps more exciting) to think of paranormal and psychic phenomena as things that happen *to you* rather than things that occur in conjunction *with you* or that actually emanate *from you.* But I would be doing a great disservice to blindly encourage mystical explanations for psychic ability and ghostly paranormal phenomena, as I will explain further on in the book.

In the first pages of *The Rational Psychic,* I will discuss the experiences that inspired a nearly thirty-year journey to understand my psychic identity. I will talk about how I learned to recognize that I was psychic and my struggle to come to terms with a sensitivity I did not even know I had. Then in great detail, I will talk about what psychic ability is by discussing what it is not, for it is very important to distinguish genuine capability from paranormal dramatics and mental illness. Next, I will discuss how the nature of reality itself supports extrasensory awareness, and how people are conditioned toward extrasensory perception. Toward the middle of the book, I will teach how to recognize real extrasensory data within your mind. I will go on to explain where psychic data comes from, some of the emotional challenges of psychic work, and why psychics really can see invisible information outside of their minds as if it were actually in the physical environment.

Discussing psychic ability is not easy. Like politics and religion, the paranormal can be highly controversial. Some of what I share will challenge the spiritually-minded seeker's emotions and the intellectual's sense of logic. For spiritual people, it is not easy to alter beliefs that secure them emotionally, while for more cerebral folks accepting that not everything is black and white can also be challenging. Regardless which side of the feeling-versus-thinking fence you find yourself on (and it may be both sides at different points throughout this book), please remember that the religious and philosophical beliefs you rely on for inner peace and personal transformation are absolutely valid. I am not saying angels or any other invisible beings you hold dear are not real. It is just that one of the points of this book is to show you that extrasensory perception is not dependent on the particulars of such belief systems.

The Rational Psychic is a tool to help guide you to your own deeper understanding of your potential. If an idea expressed in this material causes you to feel uneasy or upset, please know that you are not alone. If this happens, I invite you to look carefully at whatever triggered your emotion, as you may have encountered an important piece of information that could lead to great insight and incredible healing. Keep in mind that new ideas can be uncomfortable at first, but they can also help you create your own unique vision of what is possible.

There is just one more thing to say: although the personal stories I relate in this book are all true, I have sometimes changed the locations, names, and distinguishing details to protect the privacy of those involved. I have also omitted nearly all of my private client interactions in order to maintain the integrity of those professional relationships except where unavoidable.

Thank you for reading this book. I am excited to rationally explain for you what psychic ability is and why it is real. Whether you are psychic or just curious about paranormal phenomena, I am confident you will enjoy exploring the following pages as much as I have loved writing them for you. So let's begin!

1

THE
BEGINNING

It would be so nice if something made sense for a change.

ALICE IN WONDERLAND

hung up my cell phone and hurled it across the room where it lodged between the cushions of my couch. I do *not* want to do this, I thought. I put my hands on my hips and exhaled forcefully, attempting to calm myself by staring out my bedroom window. My breathing slowed and, as I began to focus more rationally on the issue at hand, it occurred to me I had never *really* looked at the tree outside my window. A silent moment or two passed. Mentally I was now inspecting the oak tree's bark and the texture of its leaves, all while appreciating the way the sunlight cut through its branches. It was then I noticed a curious squirrel who seemed to be studying me as well.

When I was a boy, I could watch squirrels for hours. Even now, when I need to relax I go to the park, sit in the grass, and feed the squirrels by hand. But that day I had no time to relax. I had just hung up with my literary agent. We had been discussing some suggested last-minute revisions to this manuscript, which included writing a whole lot more about my own personal experience with psychic perception. I suppose explaining how I became interested in the subject is warranted. But I never wanted to write a book about me. After all, from its conception and through its many subsequent drafts, the only intention for *The Rational Psychic* was to provide real-world answers about psychic phenomena that could inspire personal transformation in others — answers that were not readily available when I first discovered my own extrasensory ability. Upon careful consideration, however, the value of sharing my backstory has become apparent. So in this first chapter I offer you my story. My hope is to illustrate how my interest in this material began with a very powerful personal experience — an experience that may be similar to your own.

There is a good chance you and I are very alike. Perhaps you too have had paranormal experiences and would like to understand them better. Maybe you even suspect you have psychic potential. Or maybe you already are a working psychic and you want to understand and enhance your ability by learning, from a more practical point of view, how and why your talent is real. Or perhaps you are skeptical and want to investigate all this psychic stuff before you make up your mind about it. If any of these scenarios describe you, we *do* have a lot in common. And I believe this book will help you.

I want to be clear. My personal stories are not meant to "qualify" me as a psychic. Any authority I might have has resulted from years of personal practice and public service. I speak to you about my formative years only to illustrate that, despite how emotionally meaningful past paranormal experiences can be, we should never use our past as an excuse to surrender sound reasoning in the present. With this understanding, let me relate the single most profound experience of my life: one that taught me that extrasensory perception is unquestionably real, and that you and I are much more than our physical bodies.

A Very Special Delivery

When I was a kid, I had a daily paper route. For anyone who has ever delivered newspapers, you know Sunday is the toughest day. On Sunday, the paper is more than double its ordinary thickness, there are more subscribers, and the paper has to be delivered early. Needless to say, Sunday meant working more, working harder, and getting up earlier. Getting up early has never been my specialty.

One particular Sunday, however, I awoke by 6:00 a.m. without any effort. I got up, bundled my newspapers, delivered them, and made my way home in time to clean my room, make my bed, and get dressed for church with time to spare. This had *never* happened in the entire history of my newspaper delivery career. I did not know what to do with myself. So I played some darts in my room, reorganized this and that, tried to read, and basically wandered from activity to activity until finally I was just plain bored. I looked at the clock and sighed. We were not leaving for church for nearly an hour and a half. I decided to lie down and rest my eyes.

Now, the people who know me best know that I am pretty neat and tidy. Even as a kid, my bed was always made good and tight. This meant that going back to bed presented a problem. I wanted to lie down, but I did not want to muss my bed or wrinkle my church clothes. So, dressed in my Sunday best, I gingery placed myself atop my neatly made bed, arms relaxed at my sides, head on the pillow.

Before long my breathing became deep and rhythmic. I do not know how long I was "napping" when my whole body began to tingle ever so slightly. Then there was a sound I can only describe as a loud *crack* that echoed through my mind as a silent void opened up within the atmosphere around where I lay. This void was neither a dream in any conventional sense nor completely physical, yet it was experientially very real. The very next thing I remember is hearing a voice announce itself. In a firm soothing tone it said, "Do not be afraid." It was then that from within this void, a visitor appeared — backlit, concealed by shadow as he extended his hand to me.

I could see no details of the visitor's face. All that was visible was his brow ridge, his jaw, and the outline of his head and shoulders as he was concealed by a kind of muted light cast over him from behind. You would think I would have been frightened at "waking up" to a faceless ethereal visitor reaching out to me, but I felt an unbelievable comfort in this being's company, even though its presence was neither nurturing nor overtly warm.

It is important to understand that what I just described occurred at the speed of thought. It was almost as if I had closed my eyes and reopened them to see my visitor standing in a kind of doorway in the empty space above and to the left of my bed. This encounter was not a passive experience that I was merely witnessing. It was interactive and quite tactile. In fact I felt I had the choice to accept or deny the visitor's grasp. Thankfully, without hesitation, I took the being's hand and he gently lifted me from my body and guided me across what felt like an indescribable emptiness of space. I felt buoyant and emotionally detached from all physical concerns, yet all the while acutely aware of feeling myself reoriented from horizontal to vertical. The voice spoke again. He said without hesitation or emotion, "Do not be afraid. Your sister is dead." That was the message, plain and simple. There was no beating around the bush. My messenger then said one final thing to me, one word to be exact. He said, "Look," as he pointed to my right. It was then that I saw her. There was my sister.

My sister had never walked. She had spent her entire physical life in a wheelchair, dependent upon others for even the simplest of personal tasks. She required assistance to comb her hair, use the bathroom, even hold a glass to take a drink. She never really had any close friends, never had a school crush, and never had the opportunity to run and play like other children. However, what was most tragic about my sister's life was there was never a moment when she was without pain or discomfort.

By the time my sister was a teenager, she could no longer attend school because her afflictions even made sitting upright too painful. Yet despite her debilitation, my sister carried herself with a unique dignity. She never complained. She cared about others, and for her years was the wisest person I had ever known.

I would sometimes feel guilty for how much my sister suffered. We were twins, after all, and somehow my body was whole and strong while hers was severely infirm. That said, I secretly had a very unusual perspective on my sister's life: one no one else knew or, I believed, could possibly appreciate; one I have shared with only an intimate few until now.

For as long as I can remember, I've had two distinct memories about my sister and myself. The first memory is of feeling cramped inside the womb together and the second . . . well, it's of a place before our time on earth.

Since I was very young, I have carried with me a memory from a time when it seemed my twin sister and I were preparing to depart the ever-after and begin our physical life on earth. Somehow we were viewing the lives that lay before us from what seemed like some kind of precipice. I remember being side-by-side energetically, looking down from wherever, in however way we were able to see the life paths before us, when suddenly I became deeply frightened by the suffering and limitations one of the bodies waiting for us to inhabit it would impose. My secret reluctance to commit to this life was worsened by the embarrassment I felt for being afraid. My sister, however, was not afraid. In that moment of weakness, she spoke to me telepathically and said, "Don't worry; I'll take the broken one."

And so it was; we arrived two months prematurely. Ironically, I was unable to put on weight at first, but to everyone's surprise I rebounded and am still here, while the broken body my twin received is not.

So there I was that Sunday morning, caught between this life and the next, having what Dr. Raymond Moody coined an "empathetic near-death experience" (ENDE). An *empathetic* near-death experience is not the same as the more commonly known near-death experience. An ENDE is a *type* of near-death experience that coincides with a loved one's death, rather than your own. Sometimes the ENDE is just an overwhelming emotional reaction that occurs the moment a loved one dies, even though you may be miles away from the decedent. Or, as in my case, the ENDE can be a shared transcendental experience where the living person journeys into death — literally sharing the death experience of their loved one — only to return to tell the tale.

As a teenager, I had no idea there was such a thing as an ENDE nor would I have cared. I was outside my body and someone was telling me my sister was dead. As fascinating as this may sound, being out of my body is not the most important thing about this story. What is significant is what I witnessed when the messenger pointed at my sister. For the first time in my entire life, I saw her standing upright — strong in her body, her back straight — smiling directly at me, radiating absolute pride as if to say, "I did it!" For her part, she had bravely accomplished what she had come here to do. Then with a twinkle in her eye, she took off running and laughing into the afterlife.

When my sister transitioned, my heart overflowed with joy. For a few microseconds, I could literally feel the liberation and unbound elation she was experiencing. All the freedom, all the excitement, all the relief, and all that cannot be captured in words filled us as though we were one for one last time. I felt like a hundred-watt bulb lit by a million terawatts. Believe me when I tell you there are no words colorful enough to describe the magnitude of what I experienced when I saw my once-crippled sister running and laughing her way into the afterlife.

It was personally empowering for me to see that my twin had survived the transition called "death." In my heart, I knew she was free and on her way home. Tears silently fell from the corners of my eyes, sliding down my cheeks and into my ears, bringing my awareness back to my body. The messenger was gone and the vision was over. Only the paralysis common with out of-body experiences remained. My eyes fluttered open briefly and I tried to close them and go back. I wanted to see and feel again what had just happened to me. However, unlike a dream that can be resumed, my empathetic near-death experience was over. My mind was once again physically oriented. All I could do was lie there motionless and savor the experience with my eyes closed.

My bedroom door burst open. My peaceful private sanctuary was suddenly flooded with panic. I recall hearing hysterical words informing me my twin had died. As I had not yet recovered from the sleep paralysis, I did not respond. Not that I wanted to.

I was trying to maintain my link with my twin as she passed beyond the reach of my consciousness. Not knowing what I was going through at that moment, my older sister repeated herself. She told me my twin had been rushed to the hospital but was already dead.

I lay there looking at the undersides of my eyelids as if staring up from inside the depths of a deep well. It took every ounce of energy in my body to climb out of my stupor, turn my head, open my eyes, and whisper firmly, "I know."

I never cried or mourned my twin's passing in any conventional way. The events that transpired between us the moment of her passing utterly changed how I feel toward and relate to life and death. A few months after her demise, however, I was sitting alone in the house after school one day when a wave of sadness did pass over me. This sadness had been building for some time. Since I had kept my ENDE a cherished secret, I endured a lot of criticism and misunderstanding for my apparent lack of grief. But that afternoon, something or someone reached out from the beyond to affirm all was well.

When my sister had been alive she collected porcelain dolls. Bug-eyed, pasty-faced, creepy porcelain dolls. Now, in my life I have seen ghosts objectively, in conjunction with other witnesses. I have seen apparitions and I have experienced lucid dreams where dead relatives and friends have come to visit. I have had zillions of odd experiences with clients during personal readings, and I have dealt with people who believe they are possessed by the devil. I have seen, felt, and experienced things I cannot explain. Ultimately, none of these things has ever frightened me as much as my sister's doll collection.

After my sister's death, my mother collected her dolls and put them on display in the living room. That afternoon — sitting alone, feeling sad about my sister's death and for not mourning as others seemed to think I should — I began to doubt the reality of my ENDE. And, with only those awful dolls as witnesses, I cried.

I was sitting in a chair near the bay window at the front of our house. I rested my head back in the recliner and stared out the glass as tears silently fell down my face. And for the first time I said a prayer for my sister and asked for a sign that all was well. I wanted reassurance. I needed to know that I was not crazy and that what had happened the morning she had died was indeed real.

At that moment, I heard what sounded like a creepy lullaby. I turned my head slowly. One of the bug-eyed unblinking dolls seemed to stare right at me as it rotated in place while its musical stand chimed like an old-fashioned music box. A shiver ran through my body causing my arms to erupt in goose bumps. I was the only one in the house. No one, let alone I, had wound up that spooky doll. I got the message loud and clear. I said thank you for the sign, and almost immediately the doll stopped spinning. I will never forget that. It absolutely helped me believe I was not crazy after all.

Despite the apparent spirit visitation and associated out-of-body experience (OBE) the morning my sister died, it never occurred to me that my perception was any different from anyone else's. Yes, as a child I had invisible friends and a wonderful imagination. I also had other OBEs and amazing lucid dreams that occasionally were precognitive. None of these things made me exceptional — in my opinion — but the fact of the matter is, I *was* different.

In the five years after my sister's death, although I continued to have lucid dreams from time to time, and even had one very cool ghost sighting, I had not experienced anything profoundly extraordinary since her transition. For all intents and purposes, life had become normal. Until a culmination of extrasensory experiences — and the intervention of a friend who witnessed them — forced me to redefine who I was and what I believed was possible.

I was about nineteen years old and was working two jobs to make ends meet. My days were spent at a trendy record store, which was an absolute bore. But at night, I worked at a local comedy club. I was a doorman, seating guests and managing the showroom. Socializing with my coworkers after work, despite the fact I was underage, was one of the hidden perks of being employed in a bar. Since I was the youngest of the group, sometimes the girls I worked with teased me, often in ways I did not understand. Still, they always watched over me when we were out on the town. One waitress I particularly liked was Monica. She was older than the other girls and a bit of a mother hen.

Monica's Italian heritage gave her amazing deep brown eyes. She was a tough city girl with a heart of gold and a dry, cutting wit. She could size up any person or situation in a heartbeat and was not afraid to look people in the eye and tell them what was what. Believe me when I tell you, no one messed with Monica. But underneath her sometimes gruff exterior, Monica always had my best interest at heart.

She would often fill me in on things I was clueless about. She would warn me which of the girls I dated were trouble and whether particular plans I had for my life were practical. From time to time she would spontaneously share observations about how I related to the customers. I liked Monica and appreciated her insight; she cared, and I liked that. I never minded how she seemed able to see right through me — until one night, when our friendship took a turn I did not understand.

It was a Friday night and the place was packed. I was having a rough time seating the showroom because the other doorman hadn't shown up for work. Because of this, I did not have a second to breathe until everyone had been seated, the show had opened, and the girls had gotten to work serving cocktails. Before long the comics were in high gear, the audience was laughing, and everything was going well. As the drink service slowed, it started to look like what had begun as a wild night was going to be just fine after all. I smiled to myself and quietly leaned up against the wall, taking a moment to congratulate myself on a job well done. I was feeling pretty good until Monica came along and muttered something critical about me being "paternal" under her breath. I did not even know what the word *paternal* meant, but before I had a chance to ask, she walked off.

It was not uncommon for a waitress to get angry about how her section was seated. This time however, the room was packed to the point of being overfilled, and as a result I had no idea why Monica would be upset with me. So for the rest of the night, I was a little preoccupied with what I could have done to make Monica mad.

Later that evening after we closed, I finally asked Monica why she was angry. Instead of answering my question, she launched into a barrage of questions of her own.

"Did ya know those people?" Monica glared up at me from the corner of her eye as if she could see right through me.

"What people?" I asked.

Apparently I had said something that really upset a couple I had seated in her area. I hated dealing with the girls when they were mad. I especially hated it when Monica was upset. Consequently, I would do almost anything to appease her, but not this time. Whatever I was being accused of was definitely not my fault. So, Monica or no Monica, I was not going to take the blame for something I did not do. I held my ground and braced myself for the earful I was sure I was about to get. Instead of a tongue-lashing however, Monica relentlessly rephrased her question.

"What'd ya say to those people?" she asked in her distinct neighborhood accent.

Her tone was firm and her eyes were fixed on me in a penetrating gaze that was beginning to unnerve me, but I still did not know who she was talking about.

"Those people," she asserted, while nodding her head to indicate a table at the back of the showroom.

"When you sat them, you told them you had to seat them in the back instead of in their assigned seats by the stage. When they asked why, you said the rest of their party would be late because they'd gotten stopped by the cops."

I drew a blank at first, but then I remembered to whom Monica was referring. I quickly began to stammer that somebody had told me their friends had gotten a traffic ticket, so I had to change their seat assignment with another group that was on time. Monica continued staring at me, evaluating whether I was telling her the truth while I continued to plead my case. By this time, I was starting to think maybe someone had complained and that perhaps I was indeed in real trouble. I eagerly explained, at a near frantic pace, how management had yelled at me in the past for leaving stage-side seats vacant after show time. I went on to say that I had been instructed to fill the stage seats with people who came on time. Guests who came in late had to sit in the back or off to the side so they would not disturb the show, regardless of their advanced seat assignment. So, if her guests were upset, it really was not my fault.

I was now borderline freaking out. Monica was patiently waiting to speak. She shifted her weight to one side, folded her left arm across her chest, and placed her palm under her right elbow to support her cigarette hand. She took a deep drag of her smoke and as it glowed brightly, I could see a twinkle in her eye as if my distress was somehow amusing her. Monica smoked intently while I talked and talked with emotional urgency until I was out of breath and confident I had made my innocence clear. Despite everything I had said, Monica did not respond. She just continued staring at me as if looking through to my very soul.

After a long moment, Monica looked away and exhaled a steady cloud of stinky gray smoke. Her eyes thoughtfully followed the carcinogenic fog as it dissipated. Then, after a second's pause, she turned her gaze back to me and again asked, "*How* did you know those people's friends got a speeding ticket?"

I was a bit more relaxed now but still my mind was blank. I was really confused. Did I not just answer that question? Why was she doing this to me? Why was moving this table such a big deal? I was getting agitated. It had been a long night. Why was she torturing me over something so trivial? I did not know what to say, so I just stood in shock with my mouth gaping. Monica stood fast, gesturing after a second that she was waiting for my reply. Finally, in a near fit of desperation I blurted out, "They *told* me!"

Monica immediately countered, "Who? Who told you?" She was challenging me. "Who told you about the speeding ticket?" Monica scoffed, punctuating her accusation by pointing her cigarette finger at me.

At this point, I was completely stymied. Monica could barely contain her Cheshire cat smile as she plucked tobacco off the end of her tongue while she waited for my reply. She seemed to enjoy how uncomfortable she was making me. Truthfully, I did not have an answer. I had not even thought of the incident with her customers since it had occurred. They were just two of three hundred people I had interacted with that evening. I mean, I *thought* I remembered the customer telling me, as I walked him and his girlfriend into the showroom, that their companions got pulled over by the cops but that they were on their way. After all, I recalled greeting the couple at the showroom door. The gentleman then made some kind of joke about actually being a foursome as he took his girlfriend's hand. I was confused by the joke since there were only two of them, which caused the gentleman to explain that they were being joined by two friends. The next thing I remembered was envisioning a man and a woman sitting in a car while a police officer handed them a traffic ticket. With this in mind, I recalled that the man whom I was seating told me about their friends' detainment. What was the big deal if he forgot he mentioned it? Why was I getting blamed? Why was I in trouble?

I started getting worked up again as the confusion in my head began to build. I was just doing my job. It was not my fault the customers' friends got a speeding ticket that caused them to lose their good seats. I was really flustered at this point, but Monica just kept smiling and shaking her head. At first I had thought she was going to yell at me, and now she was laughing at me?

By this time I was totally stressing out and about to have a complete meltdown. Seeing my distress, Monica finally retreated. She gently patted me on the chest over my heart and said, "Don't worry babe, it's OK. Why don't you let me finish up here and we'll go get some coffee."

After work, Monica and I walked to a local diner where, over a cup of tea, we chatted about how some people are *different*. She said she had been observing me for some time because she knew that like her, I was one of the different ones. Different? Again, I did not understand.

Monica laid it out for me. The people I had seated in her section earlier that evening, she said, did *not know* that their friends were running late. More importantly, they had absolutely no way of knowing their companions had indeed gotten a speeding ticket. (This was more than a decade before cell phones and text messaging, after all.)

I thought very carefully about what Monica was telling me, but it was late and I was tired. I could feel my brow tightening up as I tried to grasp in vain what she was explaining, but I just did not understand. Then, it all became clear to me. If the couple I had seated had no way of knowing anything about their friends' traffic stop, then how did I know?

This realization struck me like a flash of lightning. I know Monica was trying to make things clear for me, but after our talk at the diner my mind was blown. There really was no way I could have known about the traffic citation. The more I thought about it the more my thoughts swirled out of control.

I felt like I was waking up inside a bizarre nightmare. I tried to figure out how this ticket business might be a misunderstanding, but there was no way to logically explain my knowledge of the traffic stop. The facts were all there. This was real. I was not dreaming no matter how surreal it felt. There was simply no way to explain how I gained advanced knowledge of something that had nothing to do with me. I had fallen down the rabbit hole, and there was no going back. My eyes were now open.

That night in the diner, Monica helped me understand I had an ability to ascertain information in an unusual way. I wish I could tell you that the first time someone suggested I was psychic changed my life for the better, but that would not be true. Learning some part of my mind could apparently perceive and then organize information into false memories without my being aware of it confused and concerned me. I am sure Monica would have been happy to help me understand myself more realistically if I had been willing to accept her guidance. But finding out I was psychic, although intriguing, frightened me. It made me feel like I had lost control over my life. To be honest, while Monica spoke that evening in the diner, my attention drifted to a disheveled homeless man who was dancing around a parking meter outside our window. His belongings were piled next to him in a collection of grimy, mismatched bags. It was freezing outside, and there were patches of dirty snow on the ground left over from a week-old storm, yet this man seemed oblivious to the cold. He just laughed and appeared to do a jig with an invisible partner, stopping only to make eye contact when begging for money from the passing drunks exiting nearby bars. I was mesmerized by his charisma. Clearly he was out of his mind, and yet in those few seconds after hearing Monica accuse me of being psychic, I could not help but wonder if this man's life was also my future.

I think my low-key reaction to being told I was psychic was not what Monica expected. I barely asked her any questions because I did not know what to say. What I heard her saying was that I had a weird way of looking at things, which caused problems. I felt condemned to be an embarrassment to myself, my friends, and my coworkers. This was not true, of course, but it was how I felt at the time.

Monica suggested I develop my psychic ability by learning to read tarot cards. She thought I would be very good at them. She withdrew a deck from her massive purse, and placed them on the table as a gift to me. They looked kind of scary, so I turned down her offer. Not long after that night, I never saw Monica again.

I am grateful Monica took the time to sit down with me those many, many years ago. It was nice to finally understand why she had always looked out for me the way she had. It was also invaluable to learn how my extrasensory perception affected my interpersonal relationships.

I did not run out and try to "be" psychic. I did not even do any research on what being psychic meant, nor did I join any classes to develop any of my supposedly natural abilities. My story is not that I discovered I was psychic and then, poof, my new life opened up for me. Life as a teenager was hard enough. I did not want to give anyone another reason to criticize me, and despite that night's evidence to the contrary, I was not sure I even *believed* in psychics. How could I consider myself one if I did not think ESP was real?

The first image of a psychic I ever saw was during my childhood while watching *The Wizard of Oz*. Remember how the traveling gypsy dupes Dorothy into closing her eyes so he can look at the photographs stashed in her basket? Well, twenty-plus years ago, when I was first told I was psychic, that scene — and some limited experience with dubious tourist-trap fortunetellers — was all I knew about being psychic. (I hadn't connected my invisible childhood companions, frequent out-of-body experiences, and deep curiosity about paranormal phenomena with actually being "psychic.") So I actually tried to distance myself from anything psychic the best I could. The hope, I suppose, was to avoid exposing myself to the humiliation of being "different." What soon became clear, however, was that it did not matter what I believed. I was who I was, and I *was* different.

Over the course of the next half-dozen years, I forgot about Monica and her psychic nonsense. It seemed that my strange perceptions had stopped. I had gotten on with my life, distracting myself with travel, relationships, and having a good time. But no matter how much fun I tried to have, or how far I traveled, I always felt a sort of emptiness within me that I now attribute to denying who I really was.

By my mid-twenties, I got caught in the trap of trying to fix myself — instead of accepting who I was and building my life from there. Each day was a struggle as I tried to be a good person while wrestling with regret, self-judgments, and the consequences of a difficult childhood. Then, while grieving the simultaneous loss of a job and a romantic relationship, I felt propelled inward to search for deeper meaning to my existence. After eighteen months of twice-daily meditation — hoping to develop some measure of inner peace — a still small voice, hidden within the chaos of my mind, awakened. From this point forward, the strange perceptions returned. This time, instead of feeling overwhelmed by what I felt and saw, something wonderful began to happen.

I cannot tell you exactly when I accepted I was a psychic person. It was a gradual process that occurred over a period of years. It required a lot of positive reinforcement and critical assessment of my personal experiences. During those early years, I had a helpful reading by a very talented psychic and spiritual counselor named Norma Smith. Norma, who was the aunt of a trusted friend, was the first person who demonstrated to me that psychic ability is real. Later, a palm reader outlined a pattern on my hand she claimed indicated I was psychic. A world-class astrologer showed me with pen and paper why my exact birth date and location predisposed me to a psychic ability. She even said I would write a highly influential book one day. Each of these experiences intrigued, supported, and influenced me in its own way.

But it was really the love of a young woman — and our little, gray baby schnauzer — that psychically awakened me by softening my heart.

Together they allowed me to glimpse my authentic self through loving and being loved.

Psychic development requires a safe environment within which to express and experience your vulnerabilities. The home I shared with my then-partner and our dog was like a chrysalis, and my psychic abilities were the butterfly. I came to trust my perceptions and my out-of-the-ordinary sensing ability through my partner. She would look at me and lovingly say, "Honey, you're not supposed to know these things about people — you freak them out." Because I trusted her so much, I was forced to reevaluate who I thought I was.

One example from that time took place at the Hollywood Hills home of an actress who had just moved from New York City. It was the middle of the day and we were getting together to discuss a project we were working on. Before long and without being asked, I found myself speaking to her about her back injury. I asked how she was feeling and shared some simple advice on how to care for it. This, in turn, led her to confide that she had been struggling. She began to reveal the very personal story that had led to her injury, and the subsequent surgeries and methods she employed to cope with the pain she suffered.

I have always had a rather informal way of engaging people, so we chatted for quite a while without either of us recognizing that I had no way of knowing about her injury and chronic pain. She confessed that what she missed most was riding horses, and that her family back east had horses. Right then a flash image of a sweaty thoroughbred raced through my mind. I cut her off mid-sentence saying, "Yes, but your family raises racehorses, not the kind of horses that you should . . ." Her demeanor changed instantly. Her posture closed off and the color drained from her face. A spark of fear flickered in her eyes. I could feel she sensed that she was in danger. My new friend was now looking at me as if I was some kind of stalker.

The actress's family did indeed raise racehorses. My knowledge of that fact made her question the many intimate details of her life and injury I seemed to know. Was I an obsessed fan? It sure looked that way. I quickly apologized and explained my accidental "knowing" ability. Slowly, she relaxed her guard and began to inquire about my psychic skills. Thankfully, she was intrigued by such things. In the end, we developed a successful working relationship.

My girlfriend often caught me in such situations — psychically putting my foot in my mouth. So I started to make a real effort to be more mindful before I spoke. I thought I had found a good way to stop attracting unwanted psychic attention, but before long, something curious began to happen. People started asking me for readings. One particular time, a perfect stranger approached me with a deck of tarot cards at a Thanksgiving dinner party requesting a reading. I had no idea what I was doing, but I closed my eyes and started reporting on the words and pictures I saw. The images turned out to have deep meaning for the stranger. Within days this person referred me to a friend, and then another and another. Then I panicked. I had found a degree of happiness through my relationship and my spiritual practices. I'd hoped it meant that my psychic sensing would stop and I could lead a normal life. But for some reason, the happier and more fulfilled I got, the more psychically sensitive I became. What kind of madness was this, I wondered.

Since it didn't seem to be going away, I decided it was time to learn more about extrasensory perception. I immersed myself in metaphysics. I read everything I could get my hands on, searching for evidence that ESP was real and information on how it worked. This was especially humbling for me. I thought I knew a thing or two about life by then, but once I began to investigate my psychic self I saw that many certainties I had taken for granted — things I had learned in school, church, and just from living life in general — were not so certain after all. I was quickly changing, and even as I wanted to grow, I also resisted. It was then I realized my pursuit of knowledge was not a search for truth. I was really looking for justification for what I *wanted* to believe, so I could retain a sense of control over my life.

I like to think my stubbornness keeps me from being too gullible. During the course of my psychic studies, I was often too proud or perhaps too afraid to really give myself over to new age thinking. Don't get me wrong, I was fascinated by what metaphysics was teaching me. I liked learning alternative views on human consciousness and personal development. I was now looking for ways to incorporate psychic ability into my life rather than conceal or kill it. But I still did not want to lose myself in what I thought of as new age mumbo jumbo.

Adopting new age thinking to explain my psychic ability just didn't feel right to me. Much of what I was learning concerning the afterlife and psychic ability seemed to be based on imaginative assumptions rather than direct experience. It all sounded like a lot of illogical old wives' tales to me, and as a result I felt a bit disenfranchised among metaphysical thinkers. In turn, I started doubting my own psychic abilities. So one morning, as I knelt down for meditation with my baby schnauzer next me, I said out loud, "OK god, if this psychic business is real, then do it again."

Immediately, in a shocking show of force, the image of a woman named Maria burst into my mind's eye. Maria, as it turned out, was the mother of a friend of mine. I had never met her and didn't even know her name. In fact, she had died years before I met my friend and he rarely spoke of her, as she'd died under suspicious circumstances. When I told my friend what I'd seen during my meditation he was astonished. Immediately following the appearance of Maria, I had a vision that depicted the deceased grandfather of another friend. This was followed by a vision of another friend's father who had died several years earlier whom I had also never met. I knew nothing of either of these men, but somehow, as in Maria's case, I was able to confirm their identities using specific details learned from observing my mind. What the hell was going on?

That night I attended a mediumship demonstration at my local metaphysical bookstore. I intended to see if the psychic demonstrating that evening was for real. If so, I had a list of questions I wanted to ask her. I was on a mission: I wanted more proof that what was going on with me was real.

I do not remember what I expected to see when psychic Jane took the stage, but I can tell you she was as unassuming as unassuming could be. Once she started working, those of us in attendance were mesmerized by her abilities. She called me up to the platform where she began speaking a laundry list of things only my twin could know. In fact I interrupted Jane more than once to prevent her from revealing things I did not want mentioned publically. After a gentle pause, Jane began sharing the very private last few moments my sister and I had shared as she crossed over. I was dumbfounded as Jane recounted my empathic near-death experience from my dead twin's point of view!

That night, I finally accepted that psychic ability was real. More than ever, I still wanted to understand how it worked in order to truly accept that *my* ability was real. I needed to know how people could see invisible things like ghosts and angels, and, more importantly, witness events like my sister's crossing-over. If someone could just explain that to me, I reasoned, I could accept that what I saw when my sister died was real and that maybe my blossoming psychic ability was genuine.

Jane had lit a fire under me. I wanted to put all of this psychic business behind me and move on with my life but I just couldn't, not until I learned how ESP worked. I made a list of serious questions whose answers I thought would satisfy my hunger. I even set a date for my epiphany.

I am not kidding! I told myself this would be my last effort to get the answers to my questions. I actually gave myself a deadline. I had a busy weekend planned, so Tuesday was the day. By Tuesday I was going to answer every question on my list. Tuesday was going to be the day I changed my life!

Tuesday afternoon I drove all over the greater Los Angeles area, bouncing from bookstore to bookstore and metaphysical center to metaphysical center, until finally I found myself standing—with growling stomach and a disgruntled attitude — in a major bookstore at my local mall. They had countless metaphysical books whose authors all seemed quite accomplished. I scanned dozens of books, but found nothing relevant to my needs. Then, finally, I picked up a hardcover by a commercially successful PhD who — according to the dust jacket — had vast experience with the paranormal. At last! I thought. This person *must* have the answers I was looking for. My hopes and mood began to rise as I flipped to the index, looking for any content about how to see angels and dead people. My eyes followed my finger as it traveled down the page until I found what I needed. Right there in the index was a listing for how to see angels!

Nearly tearing the binding to bits, I flipped to the page in question and scanned its contents. I was surprised not to see anything about angels. I expected a chapter heading, large print, a sidebar, or some kind of bold marker highlighting the subject, but I did not see anything. I double-checked the index and then flipped back to the page in question where I finally spotted a single sentence mentioning angels. It said: "Seeing angels is achieved by observing flashes of light out of the corner of your eye." I froze. I read it again, and this time I could not help muttering an expletive to myself. Was this some kind joke? Flashes of light out of the corner of your eye? I felt like a fool. I had let myself get my hopes up, only to find another old wives' tale regurgitated back at me as if it were some kind of spiritual revelation.

Please know I am not trying to disparage anyone. Writing a book is difficult, time-consuming, tedious work. Naturally there are many varying opinions on the paranormal. I was fine with hearing opinion. What I was *not* OK with was an author passing off folklore as mystically discerned fact.

I realized as I stood there that I had been looking for more than an explanation of my psychic abilities. I was looking to understand the most fundamental questions of my life. My twin suffered and died of a genetic disease. I needed to know why. Why her and not me? Was there some divine purpose to our lives — and to her death? If so, was that why I was allowed to witness her transition to the afterlife? I hadn't realized it before, but my paranormal quest was really a search for answers to the "big" questions we all ask ourselves. Who am I? Where am I going? What is my purpose, and where do I belong?

I came across that particular author's book at a time in my life when I genuinely needed answers. What I got was "flashes of light out of the corner of your eye." After reading this, I recall standing there — inside that massive bookstore surrounded by dozens of people — feeling completely alone. I knew that somewhere, someone had to have a rational explanation for paranormal and psychic phenomena. But who? I was now officially disgusted with the commercial exploits of self-proclaimed experts and I had no idea which way to turn. Science seemed dismissive of the paranormal, and spiritual writers often seemed skewed by their own personal beliefs. Could anyone out there help me understand my extrasensory experiences from a rational, objective perspective? Would I ever understand what had happened with my twin?

In the midst of my despair, something very important occurred to me that had nothing to do with the paranormal. I simply and very suddenly realized how angry I was. It did not matter what was or was not written in any book. It did not matter what any "experts" had to say. I was frustrated because I resented feeling powerless to explain what was going on in my life. Amazingly, once I correctly identified my anger, I became aware of the isolation and sadness I had been feeling for perceiving myself as different. It occurred to me that maybe, by trying to find answers to paranormal questions, I was avoiding the more difficult issues I needed to address: my feelings of loss and about love, and my question about my purpose and how to better contribute to the world around me.

My mind drifted back to the day I lost my sister. It did not matter that so much time had passed since the "angel" had lifted me from my body so I could say one last goodbye to my twin. The experience remained vivid in my mind: the shape of his torso, backlit so as to shield his face; his arm; his hand; and the tenor and steadfastness of his voice. All had stayed with me. Assuming the being who appeared to me *had been* an angel, then the author who professed angels are visible as "flashes of light in the corners of your eyes" had no idea what he or she was talking about. In that moment, I realized I should feel blessed to have had the experience I had, not angry or confused.

I quietly set the angel book down. I had just learned the biggest lesson I could have ever been taught about my life and my ENDE without ever turning another page in any book. I discovered I had the power to find my own understanding and to speak with my own voice the truth of what I knew.

Years later, I was deep into a private session where I was psychically detailing a series of events for a client I had no way of knowing. I drew a unique pattern on a legal pad, correctly identifying a series of scars hidden on her lower back. "Stop," she exclaimed. "I'm psychic too, but how are you doing this to me?" Shocked by her emotional interruption that seemed almost like a victim's cry for help, I refocused my awareness on the here and now. I could see tears in my client's eyes reflecting the light of the setting sun. I reached over and took her hand to reassure her that all was well, allowing her a moment to recover her boundaries so she might feel secure. For some people, how exposed and transparent they can feel during a psychic reading can come as a shock. Few people realize intense emotions highlight private memories, thereby attracting a psychic's attention. This means the very thing you may want kept secret is the exact thing a gifted psychic will probably see. Based on our private conversation, it seemed my client was expecting our reading to consist of metaphysical stories about past lives and soul mates. But telling imaginative feel-good tales based on esoteric beliefs that cannot be objectively verified is not a demonstration of extrasensory perception. This is a point I will reiterate throughout the following pages.

Seemingly psychic people are not exempt from misunderstanding what it is they report doing. I've devoted my life to researching and explaining how successful psychics do what they do. What I have learned I am now happy to share with you.

2

LAYING THE FOUNDATION

What is referred to as common sense usually turns out to be what
seems to be true. From a scientific perspective, what seems to
be true to most of us is based on cultural convention and may
be very different from what is true. In fact, a great many things
that are scientifically true don't make any sense at all.

ERICH GOODE

When investigating any aspect of the paranormal, the first thing
to understand is that all anomalous events conceivably occur as
an unconscious expression of the human mind. People are not separate
from their environment, meaning that human beings are almost never
just witnesses to strange phenomena. We are at some level always participating in, or perhaps even causing, the events in question. No matter
what kind of paranormal incident you are investigating — whether it
is accessing remote information, seeing a ghost, witnessing poltergeist
activity (alleged spirits that manipulate matter), or recording electronic
voice phenomena — there is an energetic coupling between the subconscious of a living person and his or her environment. So remember,
when trying to understand the basic causes and functions of psychic
ability, you must look deep within your own mind — examining your
relationship with yourself and the world around you.

What *are* extrasensory phenomena? The term "extrasensory" simply refers to those things that are outside the range of your physical senses. Examples of extrasensory "things" could include infrasound, ultrasound, infrared and ultraviolet light, as well as any information that is normally indiscernible because you are physically or temporally separated from it. An extrasensory experience is deemed *psychic* because you are using your *psyche* to register information directly, without relying on your physical sense organs.

You will hear me use the term *psychic energy* throughout this book. The term *psychic energy* can mean two things, depending on context. It may refer to the mental and emotional frequencies generated by sentient beings. Alternatively, it may also describe information that exists in energetic form. Highly sensitive people may be able to sense this psychic energy and reconstitute it into meaningful, objectively verifiable data. This "reading" of psychic energy may happen psychologically, in the mind, or somatically, in the body, depending on circumstances and the sensitivity of the individual perceiver.

Parapsychology, the field of research that examines extrasensory perception, can be defined as the study of an exchange of energetic information between human consciousness and the environment. That's right. There is a second-by-second exchange of energy between you and your surroundings. This may sound strange, but such an exchange biologically sustains you and helps you create and experience the reality within which you live. So before we jump into how information in the form of energy interfaces with you psychically, let me first give you some practical examples of how you, as a biological entity, are energetically interconnected with the physical world. Appreciating your psycho-physiological relationship with the environment is essential to speaking intelligently about paranormal phenomena.

The human body has evolved over millions of years, bathed in a sea of naturally occurring magnetic fields produced by the sun, the earth, and the rest of the cosmos.

The most obvious example of energy interacting with consciousness is that of the five physical senses. Sensory impressions are vibrations of energy that enter your physical body through a process called *transduction*. For example, your skin has nerve endings. Changes in thermal radiation and surface tension stimulate these nerve endings, creating sensations that are interpreted by your brain as pressure and temperature. Your eyes absorb light, which is biochemically transmitted to the visual cortex via the optic nerve. There, this energy is organized into images by the brain. In a similar way, hearing and smelling are nothing but reactions to energetic vibrations in the environment that are processed and interpreted by your gray matter.

Another example of your energetic connection with the environment — one few outside academia are aware of — is your internal body clock called *circadian rhythms*. Your circadian rhythms subconsciously regulate more than a hundred biological and psychological processes including your sleep-wake cycle, core temperature, hormonal secretions, and immune system just to name a few. Your body clock is synchronized with the earth's magnetic field so any energetic changes to, or interference with, your relationship to the earth's magnetic environment can affect your physical and psychological state of being.

There are a number of ways the electromagnetic environment can change — ways that you may actually be able to feel depending on your level of sensitivity. Manmade electromagnetic (EM) fields generated by appliances can pollute the environment, disturbing circadian rhythms and distorting perception. Changes in the electromagnetic environment can also occur naturally. The earth's geomagnetic (GM) field varies depending on seismic activity, how close or far away you are from the equator, and the geological makeup of the ground beneath you. The reason I want to stress how EM and GM fields naturally influence your body is because intermittent, extremely high, and especially toxic levels of these otherwise harmless radiations can affect you in a variety of spooky ways — ways the uninformed often use to justify claims they are psychic or otherwise paranormally sensitive.

Errant EM or GM fields can inspire feelings of being watched, create a sensation of an invisible presence, and even cause you to see apparitions and hear voices. Electromagnetic fields can trigger uncharacteristic agitation and aggression, if we are predisposed to such things, in ways that may cause loved ones to believe we are under the influence of spirits. In fact, nearly all paranormal sensations and events attributed to ghosts can be traced back to unusual levels of geomagnetic or manmade electromagnetic radiation. This does not mean that sensing natural energy is not helpful when investigating seemingly paranormal circumstances. With Dr. Barry E. Taff, I once psychically discerned a previously unidentified natural water source flowing under the meticulously documented, notoriously haunted Hollymont house in Los Angeles. The presence of this underground stream, coupled with nearby seismic faults (both confirmed by the U.S. Geological Service), led us to surmise that the geomagnetic activity under the home — acting in conjunction with the subconscious of the home's occupants — was the energy source for many of the strange disturbances that had occurred in the house over the years.

Now that you know the energetic environment naturally interacts with and affects your body in untold ways, is it that hard to imagine that information in the form of energy might also subconsciously impress itself upon your psyche? Think about radio, TV, and cell phone transmissions that pass through the air around you every day. This radiation is literally information in the form of energy. And while our brains are not capable of decoding inorganic transmissions the way an appliance can, it is worth speculating whether bioelectric emanations can be sensed — and subsequently interpreted — by the human mind.

As we move forward, it is important to underscore the difference between genuine extrasensory perception, the espousing of mystical beliefs, and the irrational emotional dramatics commonly mistaken for psychic ability. It will also be important to appreciate the various ways the word *paranormal* will be used. The word *paranormal* is an umbrella term that will sometimes indicate all out-of-the-ordinary events and sensations, including both legitimate extrasensory perception and experiences that are not objectively real, such as those inspired by delusional thinking, electromagnetic stimulation of the brain, and spooky psychological projections.

The term *psychic,* on the other hand, will refer to the independently verifiable ability to perceive extrasensory information. (The exception will be when the term is used in conjunction with the adverbs *supposedly, seemingly, allegedly,* or if I surround the word psychic in quotation marks. When I say someone or something is seemingly or supposedly psychic or apply quotation marks, the authenticity of the person, experience, or sensing ability we are talking about is in question.) Furthermore, I have decided to divide paranormal experiences into two categories. It is my hope that these two classifications will help distinguish genuine psychic ability ("psychic perception") from non-psychic sensations ("paranormal perception").

Psychic Perception versus Paranormal Perception

For the sake of this book, the term *extrasensory perception* (ESP) is synonymous with the terms *psychic* or *psychic perception.* I define *psychic perception* as the ability to discern objectively verifiable information without relying on the conventional physical senses. When we say something is objectively verifiable, it means the psychic perception can be independently corroborated as factually true.

The term *paranormal perception* will be used to describe the sensing of energy and information that cannot be verified as objectively real. Examples of a paranormal perception are blaming a spirit for alleged paranormal activity by anthropomorphizing your anxieties, making emotionally charged "psychic" assumptions, and espousing unsubstantiated mystical beliefs as psychic facts. Paranormal perceptions also include psychological defenses such as interpreting "energy," judging intentions, mind-reading, and sensing the unsubstantiated presence of, or receiving unverifiable messages from, ghosts, demons, or any other potentially mythological creature that cannot be independently corroborated.

One way of recognizing whether a perception is paranormal or psychic is the emotional quality and self-serving nature of the discernment. Generally speaking, genuine psychic data appears in the mind independently of emotion or belief system. For example, last night as I was shaving before a reading, I began to open my mind for service. A man's voice immediately announced itself saying, "I have a message for my granddaughter. I want to talk to my granddaughter." I agreed to "hear" these thoughts, and what followed was a series of memories I later used to verify the man's identity with my client. The details included the manner of his death, his unsavory personality and poor hygiene, a particular photograph of my client he carried in his wallet, and more. Paranormal perceptions, on the other hand, are often dramatic, emotionally loaded expressions that cannot be confirmed as objectively real.

To be fair, psychic information can sometimes fall into a gray area, where it cannot be easily or immediately corroborated. Clients frequently confirm details that came through during a private reading only after they have had a chance to digest their session and confer with family. Psychics can even be wrong. However, being wrong is not what makes a psychic impression a paranormal perception. A rule of thumb is that a paranormal perception is an emotionally charged, self-serving projection. Gray-area information will be void of personal relevance. This type of data is merely stated as fact and later proven to be either right or wrong.

Why Sensing Ghosts Is Not Necessarily Evidence of Psychic Ability

Most people who believe they can sense the presence of ghosts are interpreting their feelings rather than actual information. This is why ghost-sensing ability is most often not a genuine psychic ability because you cannot objectively prove the existence of a feeling.

Even with the most expensive instrumentation, paranormal investigators are not detecting or measuring the presence of ghosts, per se. Professional researchers who "hunt ghosts" are merely documenting the environmental conditions where people report feeling haunted. The electromagnetic environments of such places are often discovered to be conducive for creating the kinds of spooky sensations people interpret as ghost activity. With respect to using gadgetry to hunt down ghosts, since no one knows what the essence of a ghost actually is, there is no device that can detect an alleged ghost's presence.

Psychically speaking, even the ability to discern facts about a supposed ghost's identity does not empirically prove the presence of an independent, self-aware invisible person. When providing verifiable information, a credible psychic could simply be tapping into a nonlocal reservoir of energetic data he or she merely interprets as communicating with a discarnate being.

In all likelihood, the word "ghost" is an umbrella term indicating a confluence of different yet perceptually similar causes — causes that are not independent of the human being perceiving them. As most parapsychological experts agree, ghosts are either a projection of the mind or, at the very least, the result of interplay between the environment and some aspect of human consciousness. For example, as I previously indicated, it is common for a sensitive person to conceptualize a ghost when influenced by the spooky effects of a high electromagnetic field combined with his or her emotional distress. This is not to say you cannot see a ghost as if it were completely separate from you. You can. Just keep in mind the old adage, if a tree falls in a forest without you there, will it make a sound? For the tree to be heard falling there must be a reception and interpretation of concussion waves. Similarly, for a ghost to be seen, it must interact with your mind in some way.

Several years ago, I was assisting a colleague who was leading a ghost tour on a notoriously haunted ship. While my associate was speaking to our tour group, I spotted something out of the corner of my eye. Over my left shoulder, I saw a man walking toward us on a gangway in an area where visitors were not permitted. I did not want to disturb the tour, but I also did not want this man to interrupt my friend in the middle of her lecture. So I quietly turned in the intruder's direction to let him know he could not walk through. Just as I turned to face the man, he passed through the doorway into the area where we were standing and vanished right in front of me. My logical brain immediately went offline as I tried to figure out what the heck had just happened. As I stood there with my jaw slack, a security guard who had been following the ghost-man walked through the same door — stopping exactly where the man had just vanished. The guard, completely baffled, looked me straight in the face and said, "Where'd the guy go?" All I could do was shrug.

So believe me, I do not mean to suggest haunted impressions are not real, or that spooky sensations are useless during paranormal investigations. Identifying electromagnetic activity through its spooky effects on the human body can be particularly helpful in determining why occupants of an eerie place may *feel* haunted. And sensing emotional strife can help parapsychological investigators understand the interpersonal dynamics that contribute to paranormal distress. That said, interpreting location-specific emotional energy during a paranormal investigation only becomes unhelpful — and perhaps non-psychic — when a sensitive person dramatizes their perceptions according to an unsubstantiated, personal belief system.

More often than not, sensing spirits is an indication of unresolved issues within the subconscious of the perceiver. You can tell an individual is immersed in their subconscious when they "intuitively know" what the ghosts they sense want or how these ghosts feel. Think about it. Since you cannot objectively confirm what a ghost wants or feels, isn't it more logical to assume a ghost-sensing person knows what the alleged ghost wants or feels because the ghost is a product of the supposed psychic's mind?

You may notice two things about people who report knowing how ghosts feel and what their motivations are. First, you might notice a subtle self-centeredness and tendency toward controlling behavior. The second thing you might notice is that people who report that they know what ghosts think and how ghosts feel are often perceived as intrusive yet distant, defensive, and concerned about their own image. They possess an inflated sense of self and are unable to tolerate genuinely feeling their own emotions. People who are emotionally disconnected from their authentic selves can and do haunt themselves and those around them in very real ways.

Projection is defined as a form of self-deception where people see their own unconscious feelings in someone else. In the realm of the paranormal, this "someone" could be a ghost, a demon, or some other entity a sensitive person thinks they perceive. When a person uses a paranormal creature to identify and feel their own suppressed thoughts and feelings, I call this paranormal projective identification (PPD).

PPD is a process where people project any personal feelings or opinions they judge as unacceptable, threatening, or painful onto supposed spirits. I have found paranormally perceptive people are prone to unconsciously project their issues outward, creating spectral conflict as a way to safely experience their own internal strife. Thus, for many paranormally perceptive people (with an inability to discern objectively verifiable information) ghost-sensing is merely a mystical means to mitigate stress and avoid taking ownership of their true feelings. Whether such people have true psychic ability is not the issue. In sensitive people, repressed anger, sexuality, self-loathing, or the need for attention can all manifest as "ghosts" or other entities.

People who are strictly paranormally perceptive — those who claim to sense ghosts, spirits, and emotional "energy" without the ability to perceive objectively verifiable information independent of the five senses — by and large are not psychic. These types of sensitives often rationalize their perceptions as psychic, but this is so they can unconsciously process their true thoughts and emotions without actually feeling or being personally accountable for them.

Probably the most profound examples of how your subconscious can paranormally process stress are poltergeist phenomena. *Poltergeist* is a German word that means "noisy ghost." Unlike your garden-variety ghoul that is thought to be location specific, poltergeists are actually an involuntary expression of a living person's psyche — usually a means to blow off steam or act out a suppressed emotionally charged desire.

More often than not poltergeist outbreaks just create chaos. Banging noises and disembodied voices are typical during poltergeist outbreaks. But as scary as that may be to some, it is the manifestation of psychokinesis, when household items spontaneously fly across the room or vanish (called *apports*), that really sends chills up most people's spines. From an academic perspective, none of these things has anything to do with ghosts.

Your subconscious mind is capable of extraordinary things. I have witnessed people under severe psychological stress spontaneously manifest cuts and scratches that the uninformed or superstitious might think were caused by an invisible attacker. But since you and I are not separate from the environment, psychokinetic events (poltergeists) and psychosomatic issues (mentally/emotionally self-induced illnesses and wounds) are still just products of the mind.

When it comes to dealing with haunted people, especially those who identify as psychic, it is always worth considering that despite claiming to want happiness, some folks unconsciously need instability in order to get attention, resolve personal issues, or perhaps even feel normal. It may seem peculiar that some allegedly psychic people need to be haunted to get their needs met. But for individuals who grew up in chaotic or difficult households, unconsciously creating a paranormally inhospitable environment sometimes produces a familiar continuity between childhood and adulthood. For others, living in a haunted environment allows them to unconsciously work through their past while enjoying the perceived benefits of a psychic identity.

As someone who is frequently asked to help with paranormal complaints, I can say that resolving a paranormal crisis can be especially difficult when there is an alleged psychic at the epicenter. A non-psychic person looking for help with a paranormal crisis is generally more open to the idea that emotional distress is fueling their paranormal perceptions. When a client's problem is mostly perceptual, with a little love, candor, and advice their haunting is usually solved. With a paranormally sensitive person who believes they are psychic, however, resolution is usually not so easy. This is because the psychic must be willing to let go of the protective veneer their psychic persona provides in order to address the real reason they feel haunted. But the truth is many "psychic" paranormal complainants don't want help. They want recognition for being psychic.

Accepting the notion that paranormal distress is often self-generated can be a hard pill to swallow. I cannot tell you how many sensitive people resist, and even get angry at, the idea that the spirits they perceive are products of their own minds. Unfortunately, accepting the influence our subconscious can wield over our experiences is essential if we are to properly understand paranormal phenomena, including verifiable ESP.

I am not putting all psychics down. I merely want to clarify the difference between being sensitive and being truly psychic — that is, having the capacity to discern objectively verifiable extrasensory information. I am a rational psychic, after all, so when it comes to dealing with supposedly haunted situations, I am inclined to assign rational causes. Confirming the presence of ghosts (and the like) as self-aware, independent, afflicting entities that are out to get us, particularly in private residences, can make people feel like they are not in control of their lives. Rational thinking, on the other hand, dissolves paranormal perceptions through self-awareness, inspiring emotional catharsis and a sense of regained control. The kind of control that fosters an expression of a client's authentic self rather than a continued belief in an illusory psychic identity reinforced by imaginary spectral energies.

Demon in the Desert

I was on my way to investigate the home of a teenage girl named Ann. The girl's mother, Julia, believed a demon was attacking her daughter because Ann was spontaneously manifesting wounds on her body, and everyone else living in the home was experiencing horrific nightmares, banging noises, footsteps, and psychokinetic events. ("Psychokinetic" is a term that describes objects that are moving or being thrown as if by an unseen hand.)

Needless to say, Julia was desperate to chase away the supposed demon. Her desperation was magnified because she'd recently enlisted the help of a paranormal expert who swore he would root out the evil in her home. But after spending just one night at Julia's, he was so frightened he left before morning—never to be heard from again. Julia's anxiety level skyrocketed and the paranormal activity increased exponentially. After all, since the demon was powerful enough to scare away a self-described expert, Julia was terrified that she and her family were in grave danger.

With no one local left to turn to, Julia contacted my colleague Richard, despite the fact he lived more than a hundred miles away. Richard and I had never worked together before this case, but we had developed a friendship and professional respect for each other over a series of telephone conversations regarding Julia's predicament. Eventually Richard asked if I would join him in the investigation.

I drove alone through the desert communities north of Los Angeles, mentally replaying a conversation I'd had with Richard. It seemed Ann was only staying with her mother temporarily, as the girl's father had primary custody. Mother and daughter had a history of strained relations. So I wondered exactly how long these supposed attacks had been going on. Did Ann suffer the demon at her dad's, or was it only when she came to stay with her mother? I began to ponder this and other deeper questions while zipping along the dark desert highway.

It was a hot, moonless summer night and the only way I could even tell I was moving was by watching the yellow dividing-line on the road zoom under my car. The powerful hum of my car's engine was deeply relaxing, and as a result my attention began to wander. Before long, an older woman appeared within my mind's eye. Right then, however, I stopped daydreaming because I realized I was lost. I pulled over, checked my directions, hung a U-turn, and roared back the other way, worried I was going to be late. Soon the hum of the car relaxed me again, and I allowed my mind to drift out of focus.

Suddenly, a burning sensation seared its way up my sternum. The pain was so intense I was convinced I was having a heart attack. After a few seconds, the discomfort dissipated, but I had a distinct feeling something weird was happening. Then, *bang!* The pain hit my chest again, this time with greater force. My mind went blank, and at seventy miles per hour a vision flashed through my head. For a millisecond, I was staring upward from a bed, looking at the ceiling of an operating theatre. Someone was cutting through my sternum with an electric blade. Soon my chest was spread open like an animal's carcass in a slaughterhouse. I could see the underside of my ribs and all my internal organs. In a near panic, I pulled over to the shoulder.

I took a quick mental inventory of my circumstances. Things did not seem good. I had no signal on my cell phone and my chest was still burning. I had to calm myself down. A minute later, however, I realized I was fine. I reasoned that since the burning sensation was in the bone and not the soft tissue, I was not having a heart attack. Nevertheless the pain I had just experienced was so sudden and intense that it rattled me to the core.

Under normal conditions, I have a very hard time asking for help. I can be pretty stubborn and tend to suffer in silence. But there I was, alone, in the middle of the desert, having what may or may not have been some kind of heart attack. If angels or spirit guides are real, I thought, this was the time for one of them to step up and give me a hand. So I surrendered my pride, closed my eyes, and asked for guidance.

Immediately, I felt a little embarrassed. I half-imagined a bunch of guys in togas sitting on a cloud, smirking at me from the beyond. Like I said, it's hard for me to ask for help, and at that time I was on the fence as to whether spirit guides or angels were real or just some yet-to-be-explained aspect of our subconscious. So believe me when I tell you, I knew heaven must be full of people joking with each other at my expense while they decided if they were going to help me or whether they should just let me stew in my juices for ignoring them for so long. But, lo and behold, when I asked for guidance, a kind of peace came over me. It was followed by a reassurance that all was well.

I realized *I* was not having a heart attack. I was psychically experiencing a woman having heart surgery. I took a deep breath, relaxed myself, and allowed the visions associated with my phantom heart attack to return.

An image of an older woman identifying herself as "Mother" became animated in my mind's eye. With some urgency, she began showing me how she died. Soon the information in my head included details of the family I was on my way to visit. I gently made a mental request to pause this "conversation" until an appropriate time later that evening, when I was actually with the family.

Arriving at my destination, I greeted Richard and his team. Before long the investigation was underway. I had high expectations for ghoulish activity that evening. To my surprise, the most intriguing aspect of the night was observing Julia's odd behavior toward her daughter. One moment Julia would order Ann around as if she were not a person. The next moment, she would fawn over her in a display of affection that felt weirdly insincere.

When Ann resisted her mother's harsh words and invasion of her personal space, Julia verbally shut her down. After one particular exchange,

Ann's shoulders slumped and her demeanor became apathetic and compliant. It was as if Ann's life force had vanished, leaving just an empty sack of flesh and bones.

One of Richard's investigators asked if he could see the wounds made by the demon. Julia became very agitated; she started speaking very fast, looking around the room as if she were seeing something the rest of us could not. Soon she began talking about perceiving an evil presence in the room. Then, without warning, she switched gears — rushing toward Ann, as if she was going to hug her. Ann retracted her arms with her palms facing outward in a defensive posture as if protecting her face from an unruly dog. Her mother grabbed hold of her. "It's happening. It's happening. Oh my baby, they're here aren't they? I know you can feel them too," Julia cried out.

The complex, mixed emotions that flashed across Ann's face the moment her mother threw her arms around her were telling. In that instant I saw fear, pity, disgust, panic, anger, and bewilderment in Ann's face. Psychically I could feel her drowning in her mother's emotional instability as Julia energetically poured herself down her daughter's throat, choking out her individuality. Then there was an awkward stillness. Ann ceased to resist. She was listless in her mother's arms. For a moment Julia's embrace seemed genuine. I began to doubt my emotional assessment. Then the frenzy started. Julia started grabbing at Ann's clothes while twisting her by the torso, inspecting her all over before forcing her to bend over. Julia then pulled Ann's pants down to an inappropriate level, spun her around, and lifted her shirt repeatedly, as if searching for something. All along, Ann listlessly complied. I could not believe what I was seeing. Julia was man-handling her daughter like a rag doll, pulling her pants down and lifting her shirt in front of a room full of strange men. Though clearly embarrassed, Ann was completely apathetic to her mother's abuse.

Several of us looked away, while Richard intervened on the child's behalf. Just as Ann's pants were pulled back up to where they should be, Julia began to scream, "There it is. Oh my god, get the holy water!"

The hysterics were in high gear. Julia made the sign of the cross, while her youngest child retrieved the holy water. The investigators all crowded around. Ann was now sitting passively in a chair. I was not sure what was going on at first, but then I saw it with my own eyes: very slowly pink lines began appearing on the previously pristine skin of Ann's back and thigh — for no apparent reason. The lines thickened, became deeper in color, and the flesh swelled into welts, until finally the welts split open into mild bleeding abrasions in the shape of what looked like anarchy symbols.

A cloud of confusion, disbelief, and fear settled over all those watching this strange occurrence. Having never seen something quite like this before, I had a hard time believing it at first. But when the wounds were fully manifest they were undeniable. I was amazed. I took out my camera and with concealed excitement carefully photographed the abrasions. While I snapped away, there was a brief discussion concerning the metaphysical significance of the scratches. Richard stood by without saying a word. He, like me, I believe, knew it was best to let the others theorize about a spiritual course of action rather than instigate an argument.

According to Dr. Andrew Nichols, author of *Ghost Detective: Adventures of a Parapsychologist,* "hysteria is an overwhelming invasion of the conscious mind by the unconscious. It's a complex neurosis that takes a number of forms. One of the most important varieties is 'conversion hysteria,' in which mental conflicts are converted into physical symptoms."[1] The physical symptoms of hysteria can include deafness, blindness, paralysis, and even psychosomatic bleeding. Dr. Nichols continues his discussion on conversion hysteria by remarking that an "important characteristic of hysteria is hypersuggestibility."[2]

While I hid behind my camera taking pictures, I was actually giving myself a chance to think. It was really very clear there was no demon. Julia provoked her daughter's psychosomatic wounds when she used her "special" sensing ability to "feel" the demon's proximity. When she appeared to warn her daughter by telling her "I know you feel them too," Julia was really saying "You are not separate from me." Ann's wounds were not inflicted by a monster. They were a stress reaction triggered by her mother's inability to respect her daughter's physical, intellectual, and emotional boundaries. Some time later, in a private conversation on the back porch with Ann and her boyfriend, I asked her how she felt about living with her mother, and whether she had ever experienced any paranormal phenomena when living with her father.

Ann confided her life was totally normal at her dad's. She hesitated to say anything bad about her mother, but she did say Julia was always telling her to be good and not be a slut. That struck me as odd.

"Why would your mom say something like that?" I asked.

"She's always accusing me of things I don't do," Ann replied. "She doesn't even know me. I'm going back to my dad's in two days. I've only been here two weeks."

Apparently, Ann got good grades. She was rather quiet. And yes, occasionally rebellious — but understandably, given her circumstances. Overall she was just a good kid in a messed-up situation that was clearly not her fault. While we were speaking, from inside the house we heard really loud talking. Julia was telling a story about how the house was haunted. Ann looked to the ground completely embarrassed. Her boyfriend very sweetly stepped closer to her, clearly nervous about comforting her the way he wanted to in front of me.

Later that evening, when the technical team was loading up their gear, I finally had the opportunity to share the visions I experienced while speeding alone on the highway. The old woman who had appeared in my mind was Ann's deceased grandmother. I sat Ann down with her mother and a family friend. With a few other investigators as witnesses, I reinitiated my psychic connection to Grandma.

In a matter of seconds, everything I had experienced in the car flooded back into my conscious awareness. Once again, I could feel my chest open. Only this time, I was more detached from what I was seeing.

I now understood I was actually viewing Grandma's surgery — not my own innards.

I carefully observed the gruesome scene within my mind's eye. I could see the heart issues Grandma suffered and how the surgical team unexpectedly discovered the liver cancer that eventually took her life. While all this information was confirmed to be accurate by the family, it had nothing to do with Ann's alleged demons. Still, I had a hunch that the information I was getting was meant to resolve the real issue behind the supposed demonic activity within the home.

After a few more minutes of validating Grandma's life and death, it became clear to me that there was also a baby on the "other side" with Grandma — a child Julia rarely spoke of. I focused inward, trying to ascertain the cause of the child's death. I was flooded with feelings of regret. I could sense a lie surrounding the loss of this child. I took a deep breath. It was very clear I had to be careful what I said about this baby. This little one had not died of altogether natural causes.

I returned my attention back to Julia and with as much care as I could muster said, "I am being shown that Grandma has your baby. Your mother has your baby." This seemed to be the last thing Julia expected to hear. She sucked in a deep gasp of air and held it. Ann gave her mother a bewildered look. It seemed she knew nothing of this sibling. Julia then let out a sigh, took Ann's hand in hers, and asked, "Is it a boy or a girl?" I could tell she already knew the answer, but I returned my focus inward and inquired as to the sex of the baby. I saw a male child playing on a tricycle. "Grandma has your boy with her," I said. "He is loved and safe."

With that, Julia erupted into deep, uncontrollable sobs, falling into an embrace with Ann. Ann began crying, too, as she hugged her mother in return. Soon everyone in the room could feel an amazing calm and lightness in the atmosphere that had not been there moments before.

The moment Julia consciously acknowledged and emotionally released the guilt and grief she secretly held regarding the loss of her first child, a palpable change was felt within the home. There was never any invisible monster haunting this household. Julia's family was infected with toxic levels of unresolved grief, hurt, and lies exacerbated by substance abuse and emotional hysteria. The wounds Ann repeatedly suffered while staying with her mom vanished, never to reappear.

When I was young, I may have looked at my adult psychic self and thought, "that guy is crazy." But since that time, I have experienced the healing effect that comes from delivering accurate, credible psychic information. My whole perspective has changed. Practicing extrasensory perception has its risks, risks many people do not take seriously enough. So while we are on the subject of crazy, let's examine a very delicate topic few psychics like to talk about: the subject of psi, or extrasensory, phenomenon and its relationship with psychosis.

3

PSI, PSYCHOSIS,
AND PSYCHIC DEVELOPMENT

A question that sometimes drives me hazy:
am I or are the others crazy?

ALBERT EINSTEIN

Five years after finally accepting my psychic identity and working hard to understand and access it, I still felt something was missing. I had been diligently following a regimen of daily meditation, had practiced reading for dozens of acquaintances, and had devoured countless books. Eventually, I realized I had a hunger for knowledge that could not be satisfied without more hands-on experience. I wanted help measuring my progress, too — or, more to the point, I wanted assurance that I was indeed progressing.

In retrospect, I realize I was looking for someone to give me something that only comes from within: self-confidence. Every reasonable person who develops psychic ability goes through a period of insecurity. You doubt yourself; you fear rejection by your friends and family. You can't help wondering if this psychic business is worth the risk. More importantly, you want someone with some perceived authority to tell you that you and your psi ability are in fact real and valuable (*Psi* refers to psychic phenomena or powers). Although early on I was blessed to have a world-famous medium tell me I was talented — that he wanted to help train me and that I should be doing readings — it was not until something clicked inside of *me* that I began to experience self-empowerment in the form of real confidence. The kind of confidence that only comes from owning who and what you are.

Novice psychics are like teenagers in many respects. They have just enough knowledge and ability to make them feel capable, yet they can get in over their heads due to lack of experience, bravado, and an inability to weigh consequences. This became abundantly clear to me when, as a young psychic, I signed up for my first and only psychic development class at a local spiritist center. This class taught me absolutely nothing about being psychic. What it did teach me ended my search for external validation and drove me into the center of my own power.

The Development Chapel

The small chapel was barely big enough to accommodate those in attendance. I sat down on a gray folding chair next to a middle-aged woman who was wearing a polyester pantsuit. It was a hot Southern California morning, and with each new body that entered the tiny room the temperature seemed to rise exponentially. I had already become a fairly proficient psychic, but I wanted to further my training. It was time, I thought, to look for a tutor: someone who could help me gain that practical experience I could not get from reading a book or doing exercises on my own. So I didn't mind the heat. I was too excited to be taking my first psychic development class. I just knew something amazing was going to happen!

A few minutes after my arrival in the chapel, all the chairs were full. The teacher was an elderly man who, to my inexperienced eyes, looked quite impressive. The class was scheduled to last ninety minutes. The instructor passed out reading material then suggested we take a few moments to introduce ourselves and talk a little bit about why we were there. These simple introductions took more than an hour — because nearly every student in the circle took the opportunity to lament that they were either being visited by aliens or antagonized by malicious spirits.

Could there really be spirits who follow people around just to pick on them? The thought didn't sit right with me, yet these confessions were no joke. Two of the students broke down in tears, describing how ghosts routinely poked, prodded, pushed, and played tricks on them. One woman even talked about how spirits constantly criticized her, her husband, and her coworkers. I had never before heard such things. For me, it was shocking to see grown people in tears or near tears as they talked about experiences people outside that tiny room would (and probably should) dismiss as lunacy. Despite how nutty all of this may have seemed to outsiders, this kind of conversation seemed completely ordinary to everyone there — but me. I wondered what I had gotten myself into. I had no idea that a simple round of introductions could become so melancholy and dramatic.

Following the introductions, there was just enough time before the ninety-minute class was over for a rambling dissertation from the teacher — which, as far as I could tell, had no discernible conclusion. I left feeling confused and utterly exhausted.

The one upside to the class was that the study material included a great book authored by the late British medium Harry Edwards. In a matter-of-fact tone, Edwards described the need to live a normal life without setting oneself up as special or odd because of one's psychic abilities or interests. Because of the odd behavior I had witnessed, I was grateful to see such practical guidance in the course material. Otherwise the self-pity and dramatic shenanigans I'd encountered would have frightened me away. I wanted to learn methodologies for psychic development and solutions to questions I had. I was not at all interested in any metaphysical madness.

Had it not been for Edwards' clear and level-headed book, I would not have returned to the class. While I did not agree with everything in the book, Edwards' approach was grounded and logical. This excited me, because I had not encountered these qualities in most of the other psychic development books I had read. Perhaps, I reasoned, the first class just got off on the wrong foot. I decided to give it another try. After all, I wanted to learn more about what Harry Edwards had to say. Unfortunately, the class did not get any better.

For a psychic development circle to be successful, each student must be willing to set aside his or her personal wants and needs and simply be present for the good of all. Psychic aspirants must be at peace with themselves, willing to openly share their hearts and minds, free of selfish expectation. Only with an attitude of love and acceptance can a safe and harmonious psychic atmosphere blossom where it is conducive for safe exploration of the subtle, personal energies of the mind. Conversely, illogical, emotionally charged, self-absorbed dramatics can transform psychic study and experimentation into a codependent, fearbased share group.

Because of the hypersubjective nature of psychic phenomena, intelligent, patient, kind, and assertive leadership is essential for keeping any psychic development class on point. Without an experienced instructor at the helm, such a class can easily be blown off course by the emotional waves generated by students openly flexing normally hidden aspects of their psyche. Unfortunately, my early admiration of our instructor proved ill-placed. While well-meaning, our teacher was powerless at keeping the class focused. Each week the emotionally overwhelmed students would take turns hijacking the class, polluting the group with paranormal delusions.

The focus of any psychic development group should be learning to recognize and communicate accurate extrasensory information. Psychic development classes should never be a forum for paranormal antics where individuals get their emotional needs met by playing victim, rescuer, or grand wizard. Just as good parents help their children recognize and regulate their emotions by mirroring the children's internal reality, so psychic development teachers must set boundaries, model emotional stability, and demonstrate technically proficient psychic discernment for their students. If, however, a teacher fails to lead or to provide a safe haven for practice and a clear example for students to follow, the class might split into alliances according to individual emotional needs and beliefs.

When a sensitive person experiments with ESP, they make themselves emotionally and mentally vulnerable. Such an individual needs to be protected not just from ridicule or poor instruction but from themselves. Without proper nurturing and guidance, psychic aspirants may become angry, irritable, and competitive. They also frequently develop psychological defenses in the form of exotic beliefs, egotism, and manipulative behaviors to compensate for their unrecognized psychospiritual fragility. This was made obvious to me one evening when I bumped into a fellow student outside of class.

It was a Wednesday evening, and my partner at the time, Anna, and I had gone to Target with our puppy to get a few things for the house. While shopping, I spotted a woman from my development class. I grabbed Anna and, with our puppy sitting in the cart like a baby, we went over to say hello. I smiled as we approached, greeting my colleague warmly. Her reaction was not what I had expected. She was rude and dismissive, even refusing to shake Anna's hand when I introduced them. Her behavior was so bizarre that I naively thought she did not recognize me. But when I reminded her who I was, she frowned and said, "I know who you are. I heard you the first time." After a long, strange silence, we parted ways.

After that incident, I began to wonder why I was wasting my Saturday mornings away from Anna and our puppy. Experiencing the emotionally unstable, unpleasant, competitive nature of this particular class cured me of a certain naivety concerning psychically intrigued people. It began to dawn on me that not all people who get into psychic development are kind or spiritually motivated. Though benevolence is a desirable quality for psychics — because it opens their hearts and makes them more sensitive — it is not a prerequisite for an interest in the paranormal. Nor is it a necessity for making a person capable of perceiving extrasensory information. This was one of the biggest lessons I learned in that class.

The other major lesson came several classes in — after I was ready to quit the group altogether. I was sitting in the circle, wondering whether everyone who was into psychic stuff was crazy — including myself — when I was suddenly overcome with dread. I had the urge to get up and leave, but hesitated because I felt rude walking out in the middle of our meeting. Still, I had an uncanny feeling that something really bad was about to happen.

Without warning, the door to the parking lot abruptly opened. A subdued yet disheveled woman entered. I will call her Sally. Sally fidgeted slightly and then sat in an empty chair at the edge of our circle, near the door. After sitting for only about minute — and without ever really acclimating herself to the group — she, too, began telling stories about hearing voices that tormented her. Unlike the other ladies who just seemed emotionally needy, Sally had an air of confused desperation about her. It was especially troubling to me, given her hollow, nearly expressionless eyes.

When Sally joined the group, my feelings of foreboding were replaced by a sense of impending disaster. Something was very, very wrong with her. I leaned forward in my chair listening to her every word, noticing each gesture and expression on her face. She talked in circles, without ever forming a coherent thought. Finally, she began begging us for help — but help with what? She was not making sense. This was a woman in crisis.

Sally reported being afflicted by evil spirits or terrorized by voices and frightening visions. What I realized the day I encountered Sally is how often psychological distress is mistaken for paranormal activity. Such troubling perceptions may seem normal in the context of the paranormal, but anyone experiencing an emotional crisis — paranormal or otherwise — should be excluded from psychic endeavors and encouraged to seek help from qualified health-care professionals. Without proper training, it can be difficult to differentiate psychosis from psychic ability, especially when mental distress is camouflaged with metaphysical jargon. It is best to err on the side of caution.

Sadly, Sally was not directed to professional help. After she opened up about her problems, the people in the psychic development circle began laying siege to her delicate mind. One after the other, circle members talked over and piggy-backed on each other's metaphysical exhortations as they competed for Sally's attention. The group members behaved like rivals, egotistically trying to see who could help Sally the most. Each would-be psychic showered poor Sally with platitudes and hollow metaphysical principles they themselves could not elaborate on when questioned. Sally, as a result, became even more confused until eventually she appeared totally overwhelmed.

I sat quietly watching this debacle escalate, feeling as if I were stuck inside a surreal nightmare. How could no one else see how agitated and distraught Sally really was? I am sure each person who spoke meant well, but, at the same time, it really looked to me as if Sally's needs were secondary to my classmates' needs to feel heard and validated for their metaphysical "expertise." Just when I thought things could not get any worse, Sally confessed she was possessed and needed our help to get rid of the evil spirits that were tormenting her. She then told us the spirits were telling her bad things and trying to get her to hurt herself, and that she was having a hard time maintaining control. Alarms went off in my head. Fear infected the group like a virus. In a panic, two of the ladies began sending Sally "healing" energy while another prayed nervously. Others looked around the room wide-eyed, in a state of apparent shock, hoping someone would say or do something. Our ineffectual teacher just sat there quietly and did nothing.

I had been silent, but it was time to calmly interject logic. I carefully formulated my thoughts and tried to speak, but two women talked over me and a third, my "friend" from Target, shot me a scornful glance saying something sharp under her breath, making it clear my opinion was not welcome. As a result I felt like a witness who was powerless to stop a horrible car accident.

Three days later, Sally entered a metaphysical center in Santa Barbara, California, pleading for help with the voices that tormented her. It is my understanding she suffered a breakdown and became so hysterical that the center was forced to call the authorities. Sally was arrested and placed on a seventy-two hour psychiatric hold. Two days after her release, Sally's dead body was found floating in the Pacific Ocean; her death was deemed an apparent suicide.

An Unpleasant Truth

It should not come as a shock when I say that a lot of people think psychics are nuts. Statistically speaking, though, this is most certainly not true. There are, however, eccentricities among supposedly psychic people that would certainly raise eyebrows among the general population.

Delusions are false ideas people believe to be true. To be fair, everyone has suspicions from time to time that cannot be proven. But when faced with facts, healthy individuals reevaluate their beliefs. The mentally ill, however, cling to their delusios — regardless of the evidence stacked against them. For example, the other day I met a "psychic" who firmly believes a certain deceased celebrity communicates with him from beyond. While this entertainer was alive, this "psychic" had been a huge fan. Now that this celebrity is dead, the "psychic" believes he's been chosen to coauthor a book with the celebrity. *Really?* A week after I met the "psychic" who channels his favorite celebrity, I met another "psychic" who is trying to contact NASA because he believes his special powers can help protect orbiting satellites! In each of these conversations, I found myself completely in awe of the delusions I was hearing.

It may be fun to joke about psychics being nuts — until you meet someone like Sally. While certainly not all psychics are cuckoo, over the years I have met dozens of emotionally fragile people searching for deeper meaning in their lives by trying to figure out how they are metaphysically special. Whether it is by becoming a Reiki master, a tarot expert, a channeler, or a psychic, the deeper some lost souls dive into mystical pursuits the more they alienate themselves from their only sources of real fulfillment: relationships with their loved ones, their authentic selves and, ultimately, reality.

Maintaining sanity requires that our thoughts and feelings be consistent with the objective world. People who cannot demonstrate an ability to discern objectively verifiable information independent of the five physical senses — and yet call themselves psychics — show a contradiction between their beliefs and physical reality. Does this make them crazy? Not necessarily. But it is worth examining how the minds of some metaphysical enthusiasts can superficially mimic the mentally ill.

Psychic versus Psychotic

Your personality is a combination of all the unique characteristics that make you an individual. Your personality includes your attitudes, how you perceive the world, and the patterns of thoughts, feelings, and behaviors that project an organized, consistent expression of who you are under a variety of circumstances. When a "psychic" paranormally projects his or her emotional issues — interpreting their feelings as spirits or ghosts and their fears, desires, and opinions as messages from these spirits — it can be a sign that there is a potential fragmentation of the "psychic's" personality.

Richard S. Broughton, author of *Parapsychology: The Controversial Science,* references the third edition of the *Diagnostic and Statistical Manual of Mental Disorders,* published by the American Psychiatric Association, when he states a person who claims to have seen the future, reports hearing voices or seeing visions that tell him what is happening at distant locations, experiences pains that he thinks might be connected with some distant person's pain and so forth is displaying symptoms of mental disorder.[1] I had to laugh when I first read this, since I have predicted future events, accurately described client's medical conditions — sometimes over great distances — and witnessed visions that have indeed come to pass. To paraphrase what I learned here: a mentally ill person and a sound-minded psychic report having similar experiences that obviously break from what is conventionally accepted as normal. But there are perhaps four primary differences between stable-minded genuine psychics and the mentally ill.

First and foremost, properly trained psychics have control over their ability to discern objectively verifiable information. We can turn our psychic sensing mechanisms on and off by deliberately putting ourselves in a state of mental receptivity and then withdrawing from this receptive state when service is complete. Mentally ill people do not have this kind of control. They can find themselves in and out of psychotic states that can last hours, months, even years — often without ever knowing something is amiss.

The second way a genuine psychic differs from someone who is mentally ill is that a true psychic can organize extrasensory perceptions into coherent impersonal facts that can be independently validated. Psychotics, on the other hand, are usually overwhelmed by their perceptions — causing them to behave in ways that could harm themselves or others.

The third way the mentally ill differ from psychics is that properly disciplined seers can manage the emotional effects of their ability. The mentally ill, on the other hand, often need to adopt ritualistic coping behaviors or fabricate complex delusions to compensate for how their feelings and sensations conflict with reality.

Finally, what may be the most significant difference between a mentally ill person and a genuine psychic is that ill people often feel compelled to comply with the demands of their unusual perceptions. They have an irrational fear of some dreadful consequence if they do not obey. A legitimate psychic will never have such threatening thoughts.

Unfortunately, Sally was suffering from a condition far more dire than just irrational fears—it was a condition that compelled her to react to her delusions in a self-destructive way. And while the development class members were not similarly afflicted, we still have to ask, how did they come to the conclusion that they were actually psychic?

The subconscious process that caused my classmates to think they were psychic probably went something like this: the students projected their "bad" or disowned feelings outward, converting them into an imagined spirit. Since the "spirit" was associated with genuine feelings, they assumed the spirit was real. Since the spirit was real, and since they were able to sense it, the logic goes, then they *must* be psychic. Such self-affirming loops of logic are unfortunately very common in metaphysical circles.

Uninformed people underestimate the negative effects of poor psychic practice. I cannot stress enough how important a disciplined mind and proper training are for psychic aspirants. Undertaking genuine psychic development is serious business and should be joyfully respected. It is not a game.

When you observe the mind for the purpose of perceiving extrasensory information, you create a psychic chasm within your thoughts. One mind splits into two, where the observer and the observed exist as seemingly independent entities. This split mind must be reserved for use only when you are engaged in properly structured three-step extrasensory service: meaning there is a tuning-in, a retrieval of verifiable impressions, and a tuning-out where you resume your normal, unified, day-to-day thinking. This psychic self-discipline is critical, especially for hypersensitive people. So let me repeat myself: if you do not approach your psychic practice wisely—meaning you turn on, verify your evidence (using your ability only with permission to serve the well-being of others), and then shut off—you risk developing covertly coercive, emotionally damaging behaviors that can strain your nervous system, create conflict in your interpersonal relations, and predispose you to delusional thinking.

Alice in Paranormal Wonderland

Several years ago, while I was assisting a colleague during a dinner and ghost tour, a particular woman (whom we will call Alice) was irritating the other guests by instigating metaphysical debate. My friend, the host, was always very clever with how she handled these situations. Intuitively, she knew initiating disputes was Alice's way to get attention for being an alleged psychic. When Alice finally got around to asking me a rather loaded question, my colleague gently kicked me under the table to keep me from putting my foot in my mouth. Thankful for this reminder not to engage, I simply smiled and gave Alice the attention she needed.

Later that evening, while my friend was leading the ghost walk, "psychic" Alice began to act up: any chance she got, she drew attention to herself by communicating with the supposed evil spirits along the tour. At first this seemed like a harmless annoyance. But as the evening progressed, Alice's interruptions continued until finally the other guests began getting upset.

Despite the drama, I confess I found Alice's behavior curiously fascinating. The evil spirits Alice spoke to coincidentally shared not only her same attention-seeking personality, but also her demanding, manipulative behavior. My friend kept the tour moving forward, disregarding Alice's outrageous behavior — like an adult trying to bring an end to a child's temper tantrum by ignoring it. But Alice had no intention of behaving. The more the group ignored her, the more upset she reported the ghosts to be. Alice became louder and more emotional, until finally she announced that she had been called there that evening to save the spirits.

In a fit of emotion, Alice's knees buckled and she dropped to the floor hysterically. The whole tour slowed to a halt as this grown, fifty-something woman sobbed her psychic revelations to us through gasps and sniffles. Alice insisted the ghosts were speaking through her, complaining how alone and isolated they were. She herself was almost completely incapacitated by tears. By this time, the collective patience of the group had been exhausted. The other tour members were getting angry. Alice just continued to sob, unable to stand up, even with her husband's help.

Thankfully, Alice's husband, while complicit in her dramatics, noticed the group's growing disapproval. He struggled to reason with his wife in harsh whispers and tried to force her to stand. Each time he attempted to pull Alice to her feet, however, she would make a show of herself by collapsing back to the floor, channeling the ghosts, and crying hysterically. Fearing a mutiny fueled by the growing disdain the other guests had for Alice's behavior, security finally had to remove both Alice and her husband from the ghost tour.

Was Alice mentally ill? I am of course not qualified to make such an assessment. But given her polarizing behavior, emotional dramatics, and inability to discern objectively verifiable information, I am confident she was not psychic.

When dealing with someone who thinks they have an intuitive knowing ability that involves invisible beings, you never know how they will respond when you fail to validate their perceptions. In Alice's case, she emotionally cracked when her paranormal perceptions were not treated as real. Perhaps because once she was conscious of the emotions she was attempting to animate in the guise of spirits, she had no choice but to feel them herself when no one indulged her imagination. Other folks, however, are more willing or capable of taking ownership of their paranormal perceptions. Since you will not know how a person may respond to your interpretation of their potentially paranormal delusions, the best thing is to treat them with kindness. This is especially true when dealing with someone who is in the midst of a perceived paranormal crisis.

Valley of the Haunted Doll

In the fall of 2007, my colleague Dr. Barry E. Taff and I visited the home of a woman who lived in a gated community in the San Fernando Valley, just northwest of Los Angeles. The house was undergoing some minor renovation, yet, by all appearances, she, her husband, and her son from a previous relationship were managing to live there quite comfortably. The problem, as we had been told, was an ongoing and persistent verbal assault by discarnate voices. Initially, these voices had been distant and infrequent, but over time they had become crude, threatening, and sexual in nature. Eventually, the assaults escalated. The woman reported that her genitalia were being fondled by spirits.

On a cool but otherwise pleasant evening, Dr. Taff and I decided to pay the family a visit. After unloading our gear from the trunk of our car, the man of the house ushered Dr. Taff and me inside to a family room crammed with debris from the renovation. As soon as we entered the room, I felt like a tidal wave of energy had slammed into my body. I turned to Dr. Taff and in a half-mocking tone said, "This place is haunted." He had felt it too, and our instruments soon confirmed that the house contained a toxic level of electromagnetic energy.

Before long, Andrea appeared. She was a pleasant forty-something woman with a shapely figure and a strange, sensual ease to her body language. As we began talking, it became clear that Andrea's soft voice and childlike disposition contrasted with her sexual demeanor, creating an uncomfortable vibe in the room. It felt as if Andrea was a sexually precocious child whom we, as adult men, had no business being around. Had Andrea actually been a child, I would have been deeply troubled that something inappropriate had happened to her. It came as no surprise, then, when we learned that Andrea had endured childhood sexual abuse before entering a long career as an adult entertainer.

During the investigation, Andrea's attention seemed to drift absent-mindedly from person to person and subject to subject. She was never fully able to grasp what was being said, nor could she contribute meaningfully to our conversation without us having to repeatedly explain what we were talking about. Also of concern was her evident antipathy toward herself and her expectation that Dr. Taff and I would condemn her for her paranormal complaints.

Dealing with Andrea felt like dealing with a severely abused child. She seemed to have little regard for herself. She was suggestible and willing to conform to others' expectations and wishes and appeared not to have appropriate boundaries. Dr. Taff and I realized we had to speak very clearly when asking Andrea our standard battery of questions. Despite our clarity and Andrea's candidness, it was difficult to get a straight answer from her. Like a little girl who thinks she's in trouble, Andrea seemed to be trying to answer us "correctly" — rather than providing us with answers based on her personal experiences.

Andrea's home had all the trademarks of a haunted environment: a child who was seizure-prone; a husband who was frequently absent for long periods due to work; a house under repair; high EM fields; a history of physical, emotional, and sexual abuse; and financial stress. Even with all of these ingredients for a haunting present, there was still one fact that kept us from believing the home was genuinely haunted: Andrea was the only person who heard voices or reported experiencing any ghoulish activity.

When describing the sexual nature of the alleged spirit assaults, Andrea continued to speak in a soft voice and use childish words, uncharacteristic of a woman her age, to describe her private areas. She also demonstrated a surprising lack of modesty, revealing parts of her upper inner thigh nearest her intimate areas. Ghosts are not scary, as I have said, but the circumstances of Andrea's case were beginning to trouble me more and more.

When Dr. Taff left the room to take EM field measurements throughout the home, I reached into my briefcase, took out my pad and pen, and began to revisit the questionnaire we use to evaluate clients. It was then that Andrea slowly revealed more about her medical history. She confided that she had recently stopped taking certain medications at her husband's request. I asked if I could see them; thankfully, she complied.

Andrea had been diagnosed with a combination of dissociative, paranoid, and depressive disorders for which her doctor prescribed a cocktail of pharmaceuticals to regulate her brain chemistry and balance her mood. When I showed the pharmaceuticals to Dr. Taff, he quickly described their clinical applications. One of them in particular was an antipsychotic. Dr. Taff and I shared a concerned moment of silence. This seemed to point to evidence that at the heart of this particular haunting was a delicate woman who, sadly, was very ill and needed help — not the kind of help we could offer.

Without corroborating witnesses, there was no evidence of any discarnate intelligences haunting Andrea. Most likely, her paranormal perceptions resulted from exposure to high levels of electromagnetic energy brought on by the construction and electrical work being done on her home. Furthermore, I suspected that the sexual nature of Andrea's alleged spectral assault was her unconscious mind acting out deeply rooted psychological issues connected to her work in the adult entertainment industry and her childhood sexual abuse. Admittedly, not all of Andrea's complaints were sexual in nature. She also claimed she was pushed by spirits on occasion, but such complaints can be explained as neuromuscular spasms that occurred in response to her home's erratic electromagnetic environment. In the end, Dr. Taff and I advised Andrea to reevaluate with her physician her decision to discontinue her prescriptions.

Andrea was a kind and very brave woman. Her case is a strong reminder that our minds are far more powerful than most of us recognize.

Disassociation and Psychic Discernment

Disassociation is a state of mind where the subjective experience is feeling disconnected from one's emotions, body, and/or immediate surroundings. Disassociation can be as simple as letting your mind wander while performing a familiar activity like driving a car. Or disassociation can occur as a psychological defense mechanism during moments of severe stress or trauma. The effects of disassociation in response to stress can include but are not limited to: anxiety, lapses in memory, interpersonal dysfunction, chronic pain, and low self-esteem. Interestingly, these same symptoms are not unlike the issues many psychically sensitive people deal with over the course of their lives. Is it a coincidence psychic people sometimes share symptoms similar to those prone to disassociation?

The first thing a student learns when beginning psychic development is how to quiet the mind. Quieting the mind is actually developing the ability to deliberately enter a dissociative state. By disassociating from everyday thinking, you commune directly with your subconscious—the avenue through which psychic impressions travel to conscious awareness. As common and harmless as simple disassociation can be, any sort of deliberate sustained disconnection from reality carries with it some risk.

Direct access to the subconscious can be destabilizing. This is especially true for psychic hopefuls who are already hyperemotional or lack a firm grasp on reality. In fact psychic development can prove disastrous for unstable personalities. Even the most sound-minded practitioner who undertakes serious psychic development can experience irritability, self-doubt, emotional uncertainty, and an ambiguous sense of not knowing where they personally end and others begin. Thus, extrasensory devotees who practice disassociation must always be diligent. Psychic students must learn how to disconnect from the sensory information the brain uses to orient itself to physical reality, and then to reconnect to it, without losing a grip *on* reality.

When you shift attention away from normal cognitive processing and focus it on the subconscious (as we do during psychic attunement), you may be exposed to troubling information the mind has rightfully been suppressing from conscious awareness. Choosing to develop psychically is choosing to intentionally confront all the nameless, feeling-based, potentially disturbing, and repressed shames, fears, compulsions, feelings, traumas, and memories that lurk within the dungeon of your subconscious. Everything that secretly motivates you — the things you project unknowingly onto others, your childhood wounds, emotional scars, passions, pains, desires — and everything that is secretly yours will begin to have a more conscious effect on your personality. On the other hand, the self-awareness that can come from psychic development also provides an opportunity for emotional healing of those things hidden deep within the subconscious, if you are willing to do the psychospiritual work required. Unfortunately, many people searching for psychic development are actually looking for a vehicle of personal expression and aggrandizement or just a paranormal experience. Thus they fall under the self-serving spell of their paranormal perceptions and fail to care spiritually for their psyche — much to their own detriment.

When you begin psychic training, you may notice that those around you seem to be changing. But it is *you* who is changing, not the people around you. After beginning psychic development you must pay close attention to your state of mind. It is common to believe that friends, family members, your place of business, your residence, and even your dreams are haunted. Resist thinking this way. You are merely developing a feeling-based awareness of your own subconscious. You must face your demons if you are to truly know yourself. Do not let unfamiliar or frightening sensations hinder your personal development or develop into religious zealotry, a means of psychic self-validation, or worse, a self-defeating or self-aggrandizing paranoia.

In the Hot Seat

I have, on occasion, had the good fortune to appear in the media. One particular day not long ago, I was hired to promote the opening of a major Hollywood film. This required appearing on a host of radio and TV programs broadcast across North America. Whereas dealing with the press — especially fielding the same questions over and over — can be tedious and tiring, I was still excited to get started.

A limousine picked me up at my home at 4:30 a.m., and before long I was doing radio interviews via my cell phone from the back of the car. I talked and chatted to radio hosts across the country, while zipping through town to a satellite TV outlet where I would appear on a variety of morning television programs.

I was listening to one radio host bark and holler at his millions of listeners as I waited for the interview to start. Without skipping a beat, the host drew me into his tirade by saying he believed in psychic work and that he himself had tried it. He went on to say that he gave it up because it was evil, scary, and against God. Well, good morning, America! I smiled to myself — and promptly fell speechless.

Something about this guy intrigued me. Sure, he was trying to get a rise out of me, but he was not a jerk. There was a certain honest conviction in his statement that made me very curious about his experiences. After years of successfully resolving clients' seemingly diabolical issues, I understood why this hard-charging radio host might feel so strongly about his experiences. But was I supposed to explain to him, on-air, that the evil he encountered during his attempts at psychic development existed in his own mind? If I did this I was sure I would be starting an argument I could not win, in front of twenty million listeners, not to mention the fact that we only had a few moments to talk and I still had a movie to promote.

When you open the door to your subconscious via psychic development, you must be prepared to deal with what you find. You may think you are aware of what goes on inside your head, but the truth is there is a vast reservoir of unknown feelings associated with your suppressed experiences waiting to come out, all of which are capable of coloring your interpretation of reality. What is particularly influential, paranormally speaking, is early childhood stress.

As a grownup, it is rather difficult to recall what it feels like to be dependent upon someone else for survival. It's also nearly impossible to remember what it feels like to lack the language to explain — or the mental means to comprehend — how or why bad things happen. I'm sure you can imagine, however, how such dependency and helplessness could leave an ominous fear of the unknown deep within your subconscious.

Paranormal experiences can activate dormant feelings of powerlessness that stem from childhood. Powerful sense memories of infantile helplessness — the inability to predict or prevent harm — can cause even seemingly rational adults to fear imaginary paranormal forces in scary situations. Under such circumstances, people may believe they are hearing invisible cries for help — such as Alice reported on the ghost tour. More likely, such cries for help come from our own inner children, those split-off parts of ourselves that have been shut away since childhood. From what I know after many years of psychic work, there are no monsters in the ether — only the unconscious manifestations of our own minds.

Like all forms of projection, unverifiable appearances of demons, old hags, ghosts, and other paranormal impressions are perhaps best viewed as tools to better understand ourselves. This is true whether you encounter a ghost haunting the halls of a scary old building or a shadowy manifestation entering your dreams. When attempting to resolve any creepy, seemingly paranormal encounter, the most important thing to look at is how you have been culturally or philosophically conditioned to conceptualize such experiences. In large part, it is your conditioning that determines how you experience reality — whether inside of or outside of the psychic-development classroom.

4

DISSECTING
PARANORMAL EVIL

He who affirms the devil creates the devil.

ELIPHAS LEVI

had been standing in the dark for nearly two hours, shifting my weight from one foot to the other. Finally, I crouched down, assuming a more comfortable position as I faced the fact that we were in for a long night. My palms were pressed together as though in prayer and my lips pressed against my index fingers as I focused my full attention on the man lying on a mattress just an arm's length away. It was a balmy Southern California evening and my colleagues and I were in this man's home because he believed he was possessed. With any luck, the demon would show itself while we were there. But for now, it appeared the alleged evil spirit was content to only offer threats and the occasional insult, reported to us via its supposed host, Robert.

The request for help came from a local priest who described Robert as "needing assistance I cannot give." I admit my first instinct was to wonder if the good Father had first called his bishop or appropriate superior to request the rite of exorcism. After all, if he actually believed Robert was afflicted with an evil spirit, surely there were resources within the church. Nevertheless, his appeal for aid was very real. So we agreed to see if we could be of assistance.

The question of why he'd called us lingered with me. I decided to look into the matter. I discovered that in 1999 the rite of exorcism was revised by the Roman Catholic Church. The Church was now officially adamant that exorcism only be granted after supervising physicians had established that candidates for exorcism were neither physically nor mentally ill. Robert, apparently, had not been willing to be evaluated by a licensed medical professional, so the priest's hands were tied. All he could do was offer prayers and a blessing for Robert's home. After multiple blessings were performed on the ranch-style house he shared with two female roommates, Robert's paranormal problem remained.

Robert, Sarah, and Jan were all just shy of fifty years old. Jan worked a lot and had only occasionally witnessed the most basic annoyances associated with the supposed evil activity. She confirmed an occasional foul smell, accompanied by things moving from where she thought she'd left them. But, according to her these things just happen: "You sometimes misplace things."

Sarah was more vocal in her support of Robert's paranormal claims. She reported that keys had gone missing and then reappeared. Dishes, jewelry, and the remote control for the TV had all been moved, allegedly by an unseen hand. To her, there was definitely something mysterious at work. However, under closer questioning it became clear Sarah had not witnessed any paranormal activity directly. Nevertheless, she reported being a firm believer in the demonic. She described how she and her friends had psychic powers and had all sensed something amiss in the home. Together they also blessed the home repeatedly, hoping to displace the negative energy.

As my colleague inquired more specifically about how Sarah and her friends had intervened with Robert in the past, I stared vacantly at my feet, zoning out a bit. Their voices fell to a near muffle as I pulled inward and away from my physical senses in order to open myself psychically to my surroundings. Back then, before an investigation, I used to remotely scan each location, sometimes days in advance. I would record my findings and then seal them in an envelope, partly to test and strengthen my ability, and partly to impress Richard, my science-minded colleague, so he would trust me. (This was years before I began working with Dr. Taff.) While I have always been very rational in my approach, in those days I relied more heavily on psychic practices and guidance during paranormal investigations than I do today.

Slowly my eyes focused on Sarah's hands. She had coarse skin and short, thick fingers that fidgeted nervously. For a long moment my gaze remained fixed on her fingers, each of which was adorned with a ring. Then my focus softened again until her fingers disappeared into a blur. She was a large woman and was wearing a purple sweatshirt that stretched tightly over her belly. Her hands rested on her abdomen, while her ten rings glinted from the light of a nearby lamp as she continued to play with them nervously. I smiled to myself and snapped out of my psychic mode.

I tapped Richard on the arm and politely excused us from the conversation with Sarah. Richard followed me to a place near the front door where we could chat privately. On the way to the door I pulled a closed nine-by-twelve-inch manila envelope from my briefcase and, without breaking stride, handed it to my associate. Richard broke the seal and withdrew a handwritten piece of legal paper tucked inside. He studied it closely as we spoke about Robert and Sarah.

The paper Richard was reading contained my predictions about this night's investigation. Among other things listed on the document was a description of a large lady with the word "purple" underlined and the phrase "lots of rings" with a circle scribbled around it accompanied by a question mark. Richard smiled and tucked the information under his arm, studying my reaction to his ignoring my psychic accuracy. This was a game we played with each other, but we did share a mutual respect even if it was not always spoken. We then turned our attention back to Robert.

It was clear that neither Sarah nor Jan had any first-hand experiences to contribute regarding Robert's personal paranormal problems. It turned out Robert was always alone when the most dramatic events supposedly happened to him. The women did describe being present during a few minor events such as the TV turning off by itself and appliances failing unexpectedly. Nothing they reported would corroborate Robert's claims of demonic possession. In fact, living within the allegedly haunted environment only made Jan and, more particularly, Sarah potentially culpable parties to the paranormal happenings — rather than innocent bystanders. By any account and despite all good intentions, Sarah was likely reinforcing Robert's paranormal experiences in order to give herself a sense of purpose. I say this because although she was a good-hearted woman, Sarah expressed a genuine need to find meaning and focus in her life since she had a keen interest in the paranormal, no job, no commitments, and no family responsibilities of her own.

Richard and I were in agreement. Robert was alone at the epicenter of his alleged encounters with evil, and we needed to focus our investigation on him alone if we were going to get to the bottom of things. We returned to the living room and started our interview. Under direct questioning, Robert began to list all the paranormal events that had occurred to and around him. By his account, the attacks had been going on for just under two years and had gradually become worse. His claims ranged from supposed psychokinetic events such as things moving on their own and items disappearing and reappearing (apports), to disembodied voices, being pinned down in bed, and night terrors.

Richard quietly made notes while I centered myself and prepared to begin my own line of questioning. I spoke to Robert in a firm yet comforting tone, trying to subtly impress upon him that our conversation from here on out was safe and confidential. More comfortable now, Robert reported being repeatedly thrown to the ground by an unseen force. This was clearly not the case of an overactive imagination. He fought back tears as he described being sodomized by an invisible being while discarnate voices mocked, threatened, and cajoled him for secretly enjoying his rape.

The feelings of shame and powerlessness Robert experienced in response to his assaults were absolutely palpable. He would intermittently cry and shake uncontrollably as he answered our questions. I watched and listened very carefully to look for any sign of deceit. To my amazement, however, there was none. Moreover, his candid description of his personal ordeal was 100 percent consistent with what the priest had told us.

As Robert recounted his story, we sat transfixed. It was amazing to see how deeply affected he was by what had supposedly happened to him. If these attacks were indeed a fabrication of his mind or a conceptualization of a neurological problem, Robert was possibly very ill. Ill or not, I was concerned metaphysical intervention would only validate his diabolical delusions and perhaps make matters worse.

Robert told us the last attack had occurred just two days prior to our arrival. He detailed how he had been struck as if by an unseen hand, making him collapse onto the kitchen floor where he was once again violated. The only direct witness to this "demonic molestation," as Robert called it, was his black Labrador, Jinx. Apparently, the poor animal had whined and circled nervously around Robert while he was tossed, turned over, positioned, and repositioned to accommodate the will of his invisible attacker.

Robert went on to speak freely for several minutes. He provided a careful account of his attack until a flash of fear dashed across his face interrupting his recollection. His pause was ever so slight, but I could tell something had deeply frightened him. Richard and I shared a concerned glance, while Robert steadied himself with a sip from his coffee mug before he continued. Then, in what seemed to be a kind of cathartic confession, Robert painted a horrible picture of what it was like

75

to be sexually brutalized, using the language allegedly spoken by the demon. The language was much too vulgar to repeat here, but I will say the sexually violent monologue depicted a disturbingly inhumane joy at Robert's suffering.

As I sat listening to Robert's story, I could not believe this had gone on for nearly two years. Apparently it had taken months for the attacks to escalate to this level of violence. By the time things got really bad, Robert was too frightened to ask for help for fear of what others would think of him. It was only after lying helplessly on the kitchen floor following the demon's most recent withdrawal that he overcame the shame that made him afraid to ask for assistance.

Immediately following the last attack, as Robert lay on the floor with his heart pounding wildly and his lungs gasping for air, Jinx stood over him, licked his nose, and stared at him with deep caring eyes in a way only man's best friend can. At that moment Robert said he felt loved in a way he had not felt for a very long time. Jinx's affection caused him to realize he was worth more than the diabolical suffering he secretly endured. Just when Robert had opened his heart to the soothing affection of his loyal companion, an invisible force shoved the eighty-pound animal across the floor into a wall. Jinx squealed with pain. Robert could do nothing to help the poor dog because the demon returned, forcing Robert to contort violently under its power. This incident was the most brutal emasculation he had ever experienced. Robert became determined to stop the demon from hurting him or Jinx ever again.

By the time he finished telling us his story, Robert was visibly shaken. He gestured toward the kitchen as he recapped one final note, and for a brief moment I took my eyes off him. It was then I noticed that two of our assistant investigators had turned pale and were no longer taking instrument readings as they had been only moments before. These two investigators, from a local metaphysical center, seemed to drift aimlessly toward one another, unsure what to think about what Robert had just described.

Robert began to sob. There was a long silence as the tension in the room settled like dust after a strong breeze. I managed to connect my eyes to Robert's gaze and looked straight into him. I pressed my palm against his chest, over his heart, took a breath, and reassured him all was well. I asked him to talk to us about his life.

Robert went on to report a personal history of compulsive masturbation and an addiction to cocaine that cost him his former home, his marriage, and custody of his teenage daughter. He seemed oddly liberated by sharing this with me, perhaps because I neither judged nor appeared to be affected by his confession. The truth of the matter was, behind my professional veneer I found it refreshing to have a client be so forthcoming. It gave me a deeper understanding of him and, potentially, of his current situation. But the mood in the room changed, and I could tell Robert was holding something back. After all he had shared, could there be something else he was afraid to talk about? What could be more humiliating than saying a ghost raped you and that you have a problem with compulsive masturbation? Slowly Robert lifted his shirt to reveal human bite marks and random scratches on his back and the sides of his torso. "Look what they did to me," he said.

Two out of a team of six investigators walked out of the house right then and there, never to be seen again.

As is my style, I quietly nodded, pretending he had just shown me a picture of grass growing in a field. I calmly validated his emotions and reassured him all was well. Robert seemed shocked by his inability to surprise me, and as a result an odd bond began to form between us. I felt he trusted me. This was good.

Shame

I was beginning to come to the conclusion that shame was in large part the culprit for Robert's distress. There are many varieties of shame. Healthy shame is a foundation for humility. It is what gives us our humanity by enabling us to realistically accept our limitations and appreciate how perfectly imperfect we are. On the other hand, when toxic shame takes root in your psyche, you identify yourself as defective. Since toxic shame causes you to see yourself as inherently flawed, you need to create a false self within which to hide. But this false self is not your friend. It is a manifestation of your shame, inducing beliefs and compulsions. In effect, toxic shame dehumanizes you by separating you from your authentic self that is comprised of your deepest emotional needs and wishes. Once your personality is split between a shame-based aspect of yourself that feels a need to hide and the *true you* aching for love and acceptance, what can follow is an internal battle that can feel like a mythological conflict between good and evil. From this rational perspective, logic indicated Robert was not battling an evil spirit . . . or was he?

Aside from causing you to disown who you are, deeply internalized shame can foster self-loathing, compulsions, hatred, prejudice, and a variety of destructive addictions. Shame and its resulting behaviors push others away as we provoke outsiders to mirror the contempt we have for ourselves. This reinforces the delusion that we are bad and, perhaps as was possibly the case with Robert, worthy of the ghoulish punishments our subconscious mind can inflict.

Drugs and emotionally disconnected hypersexual behavior are no doubt self-destructive. But it is important to understand that such unhealthy activities are often employed by wounded people to help reduce emotional suffering. The problem is that drugs, compulsions, and other destructive behaviors reduce the emotional impact of past trauma partially by decreasing an individual's self-esteem. The destructive unconscious logic is this: if I am unworthy, then the abuse or pain inflicted upon me in the past or present is really no big deal. Once self-esteem is compromised, self-harm is all the more likely.

Manifestations of shame that can force you to self-isolate, such as Robert's compulsive sexual self-gratification and drug use, are really just attempts to hide from the pain that can lead you to reconnect with your true self. It is important to remember that regardless of what we've done, experienced, or had done to us, we are not our past. People do the best they can in accordance with what they feel. Drugs and sexually compulsive behavior may have been the only way Robert knew how to handle his deeper feelings of inadequacy and pain. In this case, Robert's paranormal conflict with an alleged demon could even be conceptualized as his own inner goodness fighting for healthy change against a demon of his own making.

The Shadow Self

If individuals are served by destructive coping behaviors, these behaviors can create a powerful temptation — one so powerful it might feel like a stalking evil force. Such temptations are not, of course, paranormal entities. They are shadowy, split-off aspects of our self, lurking in the recesses of our psyche. These parts of us are trying to fulfill our unconscious needs and suppressed desires. It is easy to see how we might mistake such disowned personal cravings as something separate from us — and perhaps diabolically powerful.

The feelings of shame, self-loathing, and powerlessness Robert projected outward as a paranormal evil were the result of debilitating guilt. This guilt fostered the demon's insistence that Robert enjoyed and even deserved to suffer. Interestingly, it also justified the destructive belief that he was victim to something other than his own mind. Thus, Robert had to surrender the idea that he deserved abuse before he could be free of his paranormal affliction.

Dealing with attachment to guilt is often the key to healing a paranormally afflicted personality. But guilt is often linked to a belief system that is quite likely both protecting and emotionally stabilizing the person who is suffering. Separating people from their guilt must be done very carefully. Clients need to trust you so you can help them develop a more realistic vision of who they are as individuals, separate from the issues that attack and threaten to consume them. The paradox here is that clients have to own what they project — the very evil they believe is trying to possess them — before they can escape its clutches. This may seem curious, but it is indeed how resolution begins.

Robert had reportedly given up narcotics and was in remission from his sexual compulsions. Perhaps he simply had not yet learned new, more effective ways of coping with stress. Lacking drugs and masturbation, could it be that Robert's stress found a paranormal outlet? Perhaps his old methods of mitigating stress through self-abuse were now being projected as a demon. Or maybe this demon was just a conceptualization of his darkest desires, acting in tandem with an undiagnosed illness. Whatever the cause for Robert's situation, he was clearly a man in emotional pain. His paranormal claims painted a very dramatic picture, but up to that point in the evening, I had seen no proof of anything supernatural.

A Night to Remember

Even when Robert revealed the cuts, bites, and scratches on his body that were allegedly put there by demons, he was playing to a tough audience. As you may recall, a few months earlier I had watched Ann, Julia's teenage daughter, manifest welts on her legs, torso, and back, which split into bleeding anarchy symbols. Robert had a long way to go to convince me a devil had a hand in his troubles. I do not mean to sound unsympathetic; after all, I had actually witnessed the wounds on that young girl form, break open, and bleed. Therefore, I had no doubt the wounds Robert showed me were not only possible, but also very real. I just had trouble buying into the demon explanation.

A skeptical reader may question the authenticity of Robert's wounds since I was not there at their genesis. This is a fair criticism, given that neurotic people have been known to engage in ritual cutting, picking, and burning of their own flesh. At times the psychotic will even inflict near-mortal wounds that leave scars. However, I did believe what Robert thought to be spontaneous wounds inflicted by demons were real. In other words, his injuries were not a case of *dermatitis artefacta*.

Dermatitis artefacta is defined as the deliberate and conscious production of self-inflicted wounds to satisfy an unconscious psychological or emotional need. Robert could have scratched himself on the middle of his own back, but it is not physically possible for him to have bitten himself there. As you can imagine, the human bite marks were highly intriguing.

My experience with Ann's anarchy symbols proved that wounds can and sometimes do erupt psychosomatically. I was inclined to believe Robert had experienced a similar event, especially because his injuries were out of reach of his hands.

Paranormalists typically view spontaneous wounds as the work of malicious ghosts or demons. D. H. Rawcliffe, author and psychical researcher, calls bloody scratches (which may or may not be self-inflicted) "neurotic excoriations." I like this term. I prefer to use it to refer to paranormal cuts and scratches because the phrase is void of the religious overtones associated with the more common term: stigmata.

At the risk of contradicting myself, I will say that among rare occurrences stigmata are somewhat common. In a religious context the term *stigmata* refers to the manifestations of Christ's wounds on the body of a devotee. But it is important to note that the phenomenon of stigmata is not a strictly religious one. In fact, in psychological circles stigmata are defined as marks or spots on the skin that bleed as a result of hysteria. Hysteria can be clinically grouped into two categories: dissociate and conversion. In the case of stigmata, we are talking about hysterical conversion. Hysterical conversion occurs when severe psychological stress is converted into physical symptoms. So, was Robert actually suffering from an emotional disorder exaggerated by the stress of losing his family, job, and home? Could unconscious shame have caused Robert to imagine that his neurotic excoriations were the result of a demon, simply to satisfy his need to punish himself? Whatever the case, something much more convincing needed to happen if I was going to believe anything demonic was afoot. Robert's ordeal was indeed traumatic and disturbing, but I needed more proof to believe he was anything more than just a good man who needed love and an education in self-acceptance and forgiveness.

After we completed our interview in the living room, Robert took us into the kitchen and then the bedroom where the alleged attacks began. The bedroom was sparse. There was a mattress on the floor; his clothes and a few belongings were neatly arranged against one wall. A closet ran the length of the opposing wall and there was an adjoining bathroom. Stereotypically, haunted homes are untidy — to be kind — and paranormally distressed individuals are found living in unkempt environments. Robert's room was extremely neat, clean, and orderly by comparison.

My colleague and I spoke briefly about how to proceed with the investigation. Robert reported being interfered with while he slept, so we decided to use a tri-field meter, an infrared video camera, and multiple audio recording devices to monitor him through the night. Robert disappeared to the bathroom to get ready for bed while we set up our instruments and took baseline electromagnetic readings of the bedroom. After a few minutes, Robert exited the bathroom wearing only a pair of loose fitting shorts. He then lay down on the mattress without any covering and tried to sleep.

We were prepared to spend the night if we needed to, but within about twenty minutes Robert reported an antagonizing presence. Much to my dismay the tri-field meter failed, leaving us with no means to measure the electromagnetic atmosphere emanating from Robert. Seeing my disappointment, a novice team member set an AC magnetometer next to Robert. This device had a sensor connected to the base unit by a two-foot cord. I did not have the heart to tell this young man that his AC magnetometer was designed to only measure man-made alternating currents. In other words, it was useless for measuring organic energies emitted by humans. Rather than embarrass the young man who was just trying to help, Richard and I decided to leave the device on the mattress next to Robert's hip, with the probe inserted under his waistband near his private area.

The room was pitch-black and deathly quiet. I leaned in and peered over the cameraman's shoulder. I could see Robert on the LCD screen. The night vision made his eyes appear to glow green as he lay completely still on the bed. I'll admit, I thought he would fall asleep any second, and within a short time I would be on my way home. But just then Robert declared that the demons were back.

According to Robert, the demons were trying to enter him. Over the next several minutes he described a conflict taking place that neither the camera nor anyone else could see or hear. He stopped narrating the invisible ordeal only when he intermittently closed his eyes to pray for help. By Robert's account, the demons were swearing, cursing him and the god to whom he was praying. They allegedly mocked Robert, calling him a little bitch and a whore, saying they were going to pull his shorts off and force themselves into him in front of all of us.

There was a long pause after Robert quoted the demons. No one dared to move. It was as if we were all holding our breath, waiting for the devil himself to appear from nowhere. Suddenly, a bright red glow lit up the room as a bloodcurdling shriek split through the silence like a wailing banshee. Holy cow! I laughed and put my hand against my chest. Richard's eyebrows were raised upward to the top of his deeply receded hairline. We had forgotten about the AC magnetometer. It had apparently reacted to an EM field that sent the device into full deflection, pinning its needle, igniting its warning light, and sounding its alarm. But as quickly as the device reacted, it was dead again.

I tried to recover my professional demeanor, but I have to admit I was glad for the opportunity to let off some steam. I knew this would make a funny story later over a late-night breakfast following our investigation. But then a rather curious idea came to me. The device on the bed was an AC magnetometer. It was designed to measure man-made electromagnetic fields only, like the kind of energy that bleeds from wall outlets or household appliances. The video camera was more than ten feet away from Robert. There were no other machines or cell phones present in the room. Since the baseline measurements showed no such EM activity and the AC magnetometer is incapable of registering the natural electromagnetic field radiating from Robert's body, what was it reacting to?

The improbability of the AC magnetometer erupting just as Robert complained about an evil presence was certainly mysterious. We decided to change the batteries and — at the suggestion of our assistants and against my better judgment — proceeded to conduct a series of experiments. For fifteen minutes, one of our assistants "communicated with the demon" by asking yes and no questions while gauging the demon's response through the AC magnetometer. While I thought the exercise was a waste of time, it did yield some interesting results. Every time Robert sensed a supposed demon attempting to fondle him, the AC magnetometer went to full deflection. When Robert felt no evil presence, the device remained inactive. This was indeed strange.

Standing in the dark, I slowly turned toward Richard. An electrical engineer by trade, he had to have some thoughts about how and why the AC magnetometer was reacting as it was. If the device were being manipulated psychokinetically by the unconscious will of Robert's mind, it meant he was potentially emitting a force capable of directly or indirectly affecting physical matter. If this were true, it would further nullify the reality of a discarnate attacker. Could this be possible? Or was there something more paranormal, something actually sinister, afoot? Not prone to jumping to such conclusions, I was eager for Richard's expertise. When our eyes finally met, he just shrugged his shoulders.

Over the next seventy-five minutes, Robert continued to describe threats of an impending invisible assault that never came. We again changed the battery in the AC magnetometer and inspected the instrument for damage. It was working perfectly. Yet each time Robert complained about being harassed or having his privates manipulated by the so-called demons, the device would go off. Could the AC magnetometer have been assaulted by invisible monsters? Perhaps. But I suspect this monster was most likely a yet understood, non-electromagnetic energy reacting to the will of Robert's unconscious and not a demon as one might religiously conceptualize.

It was now well after one in the morning and we were all getting sleepy. It was time to call it a night, but before we left I wanted a minute alone with Robert to make sure our experiments had not upset him. The last thing I ever want is to leave clients worse off than we found them.

Robert and I spoke openly for about half an hour. I shared some personal observations and asked what *he* felt would be an ideal resolution to his problems as he saw them. I wanted to get a good feel for his beliefs as well as what was important to him, spiritually speaking.

My personal beliefs were irrelevant. The best I could ever hope to do was to support Robert in a way that worked for him. Robert asked me to pray with him. I conceded, but while we shared a moment of prayer, we were interrupted by the voices again. This time, according to Robert, they were threatening *me*. Not to be deterred, I refocused Robert back to our prayers and continued. That is, until Robert began to relay the curses the supposed demonic voices were saying to me. Without so much as a nod of recognition to the filth coming out of his mouth, I continued to pray with Robert, focusing purely on that timeless part of him that was spiritually whole and psychologically balanced. My intent was never to fight any demons, only to create an atmosphere of unconditional love that would further awaken and support Robert's soul identity. It was then that Robert broke from our prayers and ran to the kitchen where he began vomiting uncontrollably into the sink. I have always wondered what it was that made him so sick. Were our prayers making him inhospitable to invisible beings? Or was it that the compassion I expressed to Robert finally made him feel safe enough to heave all his pent-up anxiety?

Robert and I ended our time together by sharing strategies to avoid the evil voices he believed he heard. On a more personal note, I assured him he was safe and loved no matter what he had done in his past. I then strongly impressed upon him his need for follow-up care with a qualified mental-health professional. Thankfully, he obliged. Six weeks later, a much happier sounding Robert called me. He reported he had a job, had experienced no further psychokinetic activity, and that he was now dating a great girl. Most of all, I was pleased Robert had found a counselor whom he liked very much. He admitted there were moments when the voices still tried to get his attention. But with the help of his therapist, he said, the voices were no longer plaguing him as they once had.

I was skeptical about how quickly Robert seemed to turn his life around but I was glad he was on the road to recovery. With the skills he learned in therapy, sobriety, a lot of positive reinforcement, a healthy outlet for his sexual energy, and a job, I am sure Robert's life will remain stress and "demon" free.

Peeling the Paranormal Onion

For many people, paranormal investigations bring to mind images of the Scooby-Doo gang tiptoeing through decrepit old houses, searching for ghosts and monsters. Watching *Scooby-Doo* on TV was fun when I was a child because at the end of each episode you always learned that "if it weren't for those meddling kids" some bad guy would have gotten away with his evil plan. It's funny because, more than three decades later, like Scooby-Doo I now believe ghouls of any kind only appear scary when we fail to understand the real motive and means of an alleged haunting.

By and large, paranormal investigators who rely on their sensitivities when searching for ghosts are looking for a self-affirming spiritual encounter. Paranormal thrills add an element of excitement to life and satisfy a need for pleasure, purpose, and attention. Paranormalists increase the level of fear and personal attention in their activities when they dramatize interactions with supposed demons or nasty ghosts.

When investigating paranormal claims, I have found it is far more effective to remain rational and refrain from dramatic assessments.

Indulging in religious metaphors or emotionally inflammatory mystical beliefs prevents paranormal investigators from being detached observers. Lack of objectivity is probably the single biggest problem with most weekend-warrior ghost hunters. This is especially true for those who rely on a presumed extrasensory ability to sense spirits.

Although Robert was a client and not an investigator, I looked for motive in his paranormal claims. Unconsciously, he may have been hoping for someone to reinforce his demonic misinterpretations in order to validate his self-abuse. This is why dealing with someone who suffers from paranormal distress can be very tricky. You must work within the client's belief system to effect positive change but you must also be careful not to exaggerate that person's circumstances by affirming any destabilizing beliefs.

Many "psychic" paranormal investigators never challenge the authenticity of a paranormal complaint because unconsciously they benefit from those who report ghoulish activity. Paranormal distress gives such "psychics" a platform to assert their alleged expertise in the form of dubious mystical discernments, or worse, to deal with their own inner needs by "psychically" fighting invisible evils or supposedly rescuing lost spirits by sending them into the "light." But if you truly wish to help "haunted" people, you must set aside your personal beliefs and avoid inadvertently using your client's circumstances for your own benefit.

When you no longer engage in the emotional dramatics of an alleged occult situation, you can become a stabilizing force of compassion and sound reasoning. This is like going to a carnival where you simply observe the rollercoaster, choosing to keep your feet firmly planted on the ground rather than get on the ride yourself. Likewise when you don't make scapegoats of emotional issues conceptualized as demons, your client's hidden motives and thought processes become more obvious. You can see demons as nothing more than carnival-like metaphors. With this kind of clarity, fear is no longer an issue and your ability to offer healing love is enhanced.

In all likelihood, conceptualizing Robert's experiences as demonic was a way for him and his roommates to understand things they were not prepared to comprehend any other way. From an outsider's more informed perspective, the "demonic" activity Robert endured was most likely an exteriorization of psychological stress. The violent attacks Robert suffered could also have been the result of an undiagnosed neuropsychiatric problem, possibly stemming from his severe cocaine abuse. When Robert told me how Jinx was thrown across the floor while Robert himself was being manhandled by the "demon" during the attack in the kitchen, this also caused me to suspect Robert may have been suffering a seizure, since a high percentage of poltergeist agents are often found to be undiagnosed epileptics.

It is very important to understand that poltergeist activity does not indicate the presence of demons or ghosts. A poltergeist event is the projection of psychokinetic energy from, and directed by, the subconscious mind of a living person. For example, to maintain proof of his own unworthiness, Robert needed to punish himself through self-abuse, isolation, and feeling unloved. When Jinx behaved affectionately toward Robert, perhaps this caused his subconscious to react violently. Maybe Robert's mind shoved Jinx away because, underneath it all, Robert did not feel worthy of being loved and valued.

Certainly Robert's situation was unusual, but was it paranormal? We may never know exactly what happened to Robert beyond the shadow of a doubt, but the truth is, most likely the chaos and torment Robert endured was of his own making.

Psychologist Steven A. Diamond says: "The daimonic [demonic] *is any natural function which has the power to take over the whole person.*"[1] Shame is one of these natural functions, according to John Bradshaw, author of *Healing the Shame That Binds You.* In this landmark book Bradshaw says, "Shame is a natural feeling that . . . monitors a person's sense of excitement and pleasure." He goes on to say, "When the feeling of shame is violated by a coercive or perfectionistic religion and culture — especially by shame-based source figures who mediate religion and culture — it becomes an all-embracing identity."[2]

The characterization of compulsions and addictions as demons does not mean there are literal entities preying upon your soul. I know it is exciting to think human beings have demonic foes trying to control us, but perhaps you and I are not really that important. It's a bit egotistical to believe we are so significant that supernatural beings are out to possess us. On the other hand, it is hard to dismiss the very real internal struggle between good and evil we all feel at times. Could this inner conflict between right and wrong really be caused by demons?

When I am confronted with an urge to go left while knowing I should go right, I am reminded of the old Bugs Bunny cartoon where Bugs has a little bunny with angel wings sitting on his right shoulder and a little carrot-smoking bunny with horns and a pointy tail sitting on his left shoulder. The cartoon's metaphor is not far from the truth. Human beings (and cartoon rabbits, apparently) literally have a dual consciousness. According to Michael Gazzaniga and Joseph LeDoux, authors of *The Integrated Mind,* research has shown each hemisphere of the brain does more than just serve important perceptual functions. Each hemisphere actually creates separate consciousnesses that function independently of one another.[3] Every single person can experience one of two very different interpretations of reality, depending on whether he or she is operating through the left or right hemisphere. To clarify, the right side of your brain deals with the world spatially through feelings, imagination, and creativity, while the left side serves the linear functions of analytical thought and language.

Under normal circumstances, right- and left-brain-inspired consciousnesses complement each other, creating one cohesive view of reality. When threatened or under stress, a survival mechanism can temporarily suppress the right brain, making you entirely left-brained. The result is people have an increased capability to act in their own self-interest, unimpeded by the wants or needs of others. In other words, where normally an integrated right-left brain consciousness supports a willingness to cooperate with other people, under stress we are wired to focus specifically on our own survival.

The change in our perceptual processing I just described can be immediate and dramatic. It can be so dramatic that our very beliefs, and in some cases even our morals, may shift, making it possible to behave in ways that seem counter to our personality. It is my suspicion that this inner temptation to behave selfishly, and counter to our "normal self," might cause some people to reason they have fallen under the influence of a demon. Neurologically speaking then, we *do* have a metaphorical angel on one shoulder and devil on the other. The difference is they are not actual entities and aren't separate from who we are. The devil and/or angel you may feel prodding you are merely different aspects of your mind functioning from different perceptual points of view.

The temptations people face — whether psychological, physical, or chemical — only feel paranormally inspired when we deny ownership of our issues. There are no demons that see into your mind, attempting to use your vulnerabilities against you. Alleged evil spirits only know your secrets and vulnerabilities because they are actually you!

Exorcist, author, and former Jesuit priest Malachi Martin explains in his book *Hostage to the Devil* that possession is an ongoing process. He describes it as "a process that affects the two faculties of the soul: the mind, by which an individual receives and internalizes knowledge. And the will, by which an individual chooses to act upon that knowledge."[4] Nonetheless, even if you believe in demons as individual sentient creatures, their influence over you still requires you to choose to submit both your will and your intellect to their control. Thus, the power over internal and external supernatural evil, if it even exists, still rests within your mind.

I do not believe demons are anything more than a means to avoid personal accountability for one's thoughts, desires, and actions. Whatever the animating principle of consciousness, whatever the creative force behind the ever-evolving order of the universe, it is perfect. Whether we call it god, consciousness, intelligent design, or cosmos, only the limited scope of human understanding fragments the universe into notions of good and evil. Yes, the universe is a counterbalance of opposites, but only within the context of human preferences can anything (including those things deemed paranormal) actually be "good" or "evil." Paranormal manifestations are simply expressions of the same, yet-to-be-understood creative source all manner of natural life and phenomena spring from. Despite appearances, seemingly demonic and other paranormal events actually have no intrinsic moral character of their own other than that which we supply.

The Real Origin of the Word *Demon*

Owning our mental and emotional suffering affords us the ability to find solutions to our problems without fearing supernatural conflict. For this reason alone, it is helpful to view demons as metaphors that represent inner strife rather than literal beings that torment us. I am not asking you to give up your religion. If you are a religious person, I encourage you to avail yourself of the divine as a way to acquire healing grace. All I am suggesting is that understanding how we've been conditioned to conceptualize our inner life as potential afflicting diabolical forces actually keeps us from experiencing the true essence of our being in relation to what we may conceive of as holy.

The English word *demon* has its origin in 1387 AD. It was adapted from the Latin phrase "daemon spirit," which came from the Greek word *daimon* meaning "lesser god" or, more appropriate for this discussion, "guiding spirit" or "indwelling spirit."

The Greek philosopher Plato described Socrates's relationship with his daemon (indwelling spirit) by saying that Socrates would go into deep contemplation for hours (and sometimes days) consulting his guiding spirit. When I hear the story of Socrates, it reminds me of Jesus meditating in the garden of Gethsemane. I also think of Prince

Siddhartha sitting in meditation, which led to his enlightenment as the Buddha, and the stories of Moses and Abraham communing similarly with Jehovah. Taking into consideration how each of these great religious figures attuned themselves to an inner guidance system which enabled them to be the blessing they were to humanity, it is difficult to understand how modern people have come to imagine there is an invisible evil within. By understanding the original definition of the word "demon," however, perhaps we can speculate how modern man has learned to fear and project inner states of being. Could it be that historical rulers redefined the term *demon* to dissuade individuals from embracing their personal power — a power within all of us that is similar to what Jesus, Abraham, Krishna, and the Buddha discovered?

For the purpose of understanding how modern people have learned to use the word demon to describe troubling physical sensations and mental as well as emotional experiences, let's examine the historical influence the Roman culture had on Western civilization. Prior to Judeo-Christian influence, most civilizations were polytheistic. This means people believed there were many gods; one god who governed each of the physical or immaterial aspects that influenced human life. Polytheism was extremely practical for a pagan superpower like Rome. People who lived to please gods that existed outside of themselves were conditioned through their religious practices to surrender personal power to external forces. Since Roman culture accepted the idea of multiple gods, whenever Rome conquered a new civilization the Romans simply absorbed that society's religious customs into their own. This model of conquering, first by force and then by annexing religious beliefs, worked in every single instance except when Rome conquered Israel.

The Romans were never able to fully integrate the Jews into Roman society because the Jews believed in one supreme god rather than many gods like the other cultures Rome had conquered. For Rome to govern the Jews peacefully, they had to let the Jews keep their traditions. This meant striking an agreement with the chief priests of the Hebrew temple. The Jews were allowed to remain semi-autonomous so long as their religious leaders cooperated with the emperor by enforcing Roman will. This style of government worked fairly well until Jesus started teaching the Jews that god was within each man, rather than inside the temple. By spiritually empowering individual citizens, Jesus upset the social and political order of the entire Roman Empire. We all know what happened to Jesus. Nevertheless, his teachings lived on.

By 300 AD, this "heaven is within" business Jesus started had spread throughout Roman civilization, leading to widespread social unrest and religious persecution. Eventually, the disruption caused by Christianity threatened to tear apart the social fabric of Roman society. After the emperor Constantine's own mother converted to Christianity, he himself became Christian. Whether Constantine converted to Christianity for philosophical reasons or simply because it was good politics is a matter for another discussion. Either way, Christianity was legalized by Constantine in 313 AD.

For Christians, the ability to practice freely without fear of persecution was a blessing, but this freedom also came at a philosophical price. Following Constantine's conversion, the resulting symbiotic relationship between the early Christian church and the Roman Empire arguably changed Christianity from the contemplative inward spiritual journey Jesus taught — which liberated individuals from religious governance — to a religion that once again taught that the word of god came not from within, but from the mouths of church leaders. Eventually, in an effort to consolidate power, the Roman government declared that anyone who espoused beliefs or participated in practices not sanctioned by the official Church of Rome was colluding with the devil. With the adoption of the devil as a tool of coercion, people's personal convictions and spiritual intuition became evidence of demonic influence. Thus, the historical definition of the word *demon* was changed forever. Once a term used by Socrates to denote a benevolent, guiding, indwelling intelligence — not unlike personal intuition or the Holy Spirit — *daimon* was now corrupted to mean an evil spirit to be feared and avoided. After all, people who go within for answers are harder to control than people who depend on the government to solve their problems.

A Modern Metaphysical Mystery

Although the subtle perversion of one's internal guidance into something potentially evil occurred during Rome's dominance over Western civilization, it really was not until the fifth century when the term *daemon* became fully corrupted. It was at this time that a doctor first suggested that neurotic women could be driven mad, even to suicide, by evil daemons. Why would a seemingly educated man pose such a theory? Perhaps in such a paternalistic society it was easier to scapegoat invisible spirits rather than address gender inequality and scientific ignorance. Instead it was much easier to assume suicidal woman were simply the sad result of an inexplicable interplay between our world and the spirit world.

Modern metaphysics also promotes the idea that there is an inhabited spiritual reality coexisting with physical reality. Exploring this boundary between the seen and unseen world is what paranormal enthusiasts find so exciting. Until you appreciate that most metaphysical and paranormal concepts are only metaphors, any deeper understanding of parapsychology — and yourself in relation to a spiritual reality — is next to impossible.

The paranormal as an extension of metaphysics presupposes there are multiple possible realities. This may sound outrageous, but quantum physics also supports this idea. Even neuroscience asserts there are at least two realities existing simultaneously. The first reality neuroscience acknowledges is the objective physical world, and the second is the subjective world within our brains where we interpret sense perceptions into experience.

As discussed in Chapter 2, we internalize the physical world through a process called transduction. As a reminder, transduction is the method through which environmental vibrations of light, sound, smell, and touch are absorbed through nerve endings in our eyes, ears, nose, and skin. After they are absorbed, these vibrations are converted into chemical neurotransmitters that are sent to the brain. Once inside the brain, sense perceptions are organized and assigned meaning through association with memory and emotion.

What happens if the brain cannot logically compute what it perceives? What if it cannot assign meaning, comprehend a recognizable pattern, or determine cause and effect? This inability to order our experiences rationally — based on what we have learned and accepted as real — is, in short, how we come to characterize an experience as paranormal.

Over the course of human history, as mankind has educated itself on how the natural world functions, things that were once considered supernatural have become ordinary. We only have to look at different cultures' folklore, ancient religions, and even some modern belief systems to recognize how myths have long been used to explain seemingly paranormal things. When I say something is a myth, I don't mean it is a construct of the imagination. Myths are powerful metaphors that help explain life's mysteries. Such myths include the afterlife, the origin of man, human nature, and morality.

There are two brain functions that are primarily responsible for the creation of myth: the binary and causal operators. The binary operator recognizes information in terms of opposites, like up and down, black and white, or good and evil. These fixed opposites help us orient ourselves in our virtual world. At the same time, the brain's causal operator supplies the reasoning for *why* we perceive reality as it appears to be. This kind of causal reasoning does not have to be factual. It only needs to *feel logical* to seem real. It is for this reason the causal operator loves myth; myth explains the inexplicable in the simplest of terms and in accordance with what feels right, not what is necessarily factual.

My very good friend and colleague Dr. Barry Taff is a bit of a genius. As such, he can speak right to the heart of a matter — illuminating the ridiculous, much to the chagrin of the person or people he is speaking with. Once upon a time, Dr. Taff was working on a TV production at an alleged haunted house. During this engagement, the television crew kept prompting him to speak about demons and the possibility they were lurking on the property. He refused. There were two other "experts" hired by the production, however, who were quite eager to discuss their demonic findings. These other experts were an eccentric yet earnest husband-and-wife ghost-busting team armed with a vast array of devices that had absolutely no parapsychological value.

While the cameras rolled, the husband referred to an electrostatic globe that looked like a prop from an old Frankenstein movie. He said that ghosts and demons were attracted to the "novelty sphere" because they liked it. How the man determined the actual presence of "ghosts" and the idea his invisible visitors liked his globe remains a ridiculous mystery. However, once the device was switched on, the wife claimed she could talk to the ghosts who gathered around the electrostatic globe; so I guess they told her. Needless to say, the television crew ate this nonsense up. The hijinks continued for several more minutes as the globe crackled and popped, punctuating one ridiculous statement after the next, while Dr. Taff sat shaking his head in his hands. As the cameraman zoomed in for a close-up shot of the arching static ball, the wife began channeling an alleged demon she thought was haunting the property. "It is evil," she declared. "It is evil," she said over and over again, swaying back and forth as if she were in a trance. The lead TV producer quickly gestured to the cameras to switch their focus to the wife.

Dr. Taff could not bite his tongue any longer. He had already demonstrated the most serious problem with the property was extreme geomagnetic activity, which was also confirmed by the US Geological Service.

"It is evil," the wife continued in a melancholy, trancelike voice. "It is evil. It wants to . . ." The producers were getting excited because this was exactly the kind of footage they had hoped for. The lead producer encouraged the woman to continue by asking her what the ghosts were saying. "It is evil," she stated again.

Dr. Taff finally broke in, "How do you know what you are sensing is evil?"

"Because ghosts with evil energy make me feel sick," she replied with indignant psychic certainty.

"Well of course you are feeling sick," Dr. Taff calmly replied. "You are standing on a fault in the earth's crust that is emitting high levels of geomagnetic radiation. If it gave you an orgasm, would you think it was an angel?"

Strange beliefs do not necessarily make you crazy. Even grounded, rational people sometimes rely on spiritual metaphors to help explain things they do not understand. It is only when you cling to unfounded beliefs in the face of facts that your sanity might come into question. Mythologically speaking, demons are extremely useful. They explain the often illogical nature of evil people, random tragedies, and why good people sometimes do bad things. But again, just because mythological demons serve a valuable purpose, it does not make them factual.

The tendency to blame invisible creatures for temptations, changes in your mood, or shame-inducing thoughts and actions could come from a misunderstanding of your mind's relationship with the environment. Later on I will discuss how information is theoretically expressed by the body and impressed within the environment, but for right now let's look at how a natural sensitivity to such information might influence you in ways that might seem to be caused by an invisible evil.

It is not uncommon to feel ill at ease in the company of certain people. Haven't you ever encountered a stranger who just makes your skin crawl without understanding why? Imagine what a pristine chapel feels like versus a filthy chaotic subway station. Or imagine how, when in the company of a depressed friend you might doubt your own self-worth. Maybe after listening to a colleague lament about their marriage, you begin to fear for your own relationship. What I am suggesting here is that even when we are not conscious of the effects we have on one another, the mental and emotional energy we emit is palpable, can stay within the environment, and does affect us. The only cure for this kind of passive receptivity is keen, clear self-awareness and a willful assertion of our individuality.

Many beliefs associated with modern metaphysics that are used to explain the alleged paranormal aspects of reality have their roots in a movement that dates back to the latter part of the nineteenth century. This movement was called Theosophy. Theosophy is a collage of beliefs including Christian, Hindu, and Buddhist mythology as well as theories from Spiritualism, yoga, and basically any and all philosophies that explain the nature of reality and life after death. Following the death of Helena Blavatsky, one of Theosophy's founders, the movement was spread through two of its most famous members and authors, Annie Besant and former Church of England clergyman, Charles W. Leadbeater.

Leadbeater and Besant, along with their Theosophist colleagues, published dozens of books, magazines, and journals. An interesting practice carried out by Theosophists was their use of clairvoyance to examine, explore, and conceive of the many esoteric teachings they espoused.

According to the Theosophists, what sensitive individuals who feel tempted by spirits are most likely reacting to (if not their own imaginations) are *thought forms.* Leadbeater and Besant explain the effect thought forms can have on your mind in one of their books — conveniently titled *Thought Forms.*

> If a man's thought is about himself, or is based upon a personal feeling, as the vast majority of thoughts are, it hovers around its creator and is always ready to react upon him whenever he is for a moment in a passive condition. For example, a man who yields himself to thoughts of impurity may forget all about them while he is engaged in the daily routine of business, even though the resultant forms are hanging round him in a heavy cloud,

because his attention is otherwise directed and his astral body is therefore not impressible by any other rate of vibration than its own. When, however, the marked vibration slackens and the man rests after his labors and leaves his mind blank as regards definite thought, he is very likely to feel the vibrations of impurity stealing insidiously upon him. If the consciousness of the man be to any extent awakened, he may perceive this and cry out that he is being tempted by the devil; yet the truth is that the temptation is from without only in appearance, since it is nothing but the natural reaction upon him of his own thought-forms.[5]

Thought forms are self-created. Regardless of external conceptualizations, you alone are responsible for your mind and your well-being.

Recently, I attended an unconventional Spiritualist church. Spiritualist churches typically rely on technically proficient, approved lay people or ordained ministers as their mediums. According to tradition, it is the responsibility of the medium to demonstrate a continuation of life after death by conveying verifiable extrasensory information. This particular church, however, did not have properly trained mediums capable of demonstrating the discernment of objectively verifiable information. Without a credible medium to serve the congregation by providing messages, this church claimed to be primarily a spiritual healing ministry. Their healing mission, I was told, was to remove spirits from within people. To justify this mission, the pastor himself claimed to have a spirit within. Was this a case of the blind leading the blind?

In a private conversation with the pastor, where he professed to "talking" spirits out of countless people, I expressed concern that his philosophy might inflict real emotional trauma upon vulnerable minds looking to him for spiritual guidance. When I suggested this, I could not help noticing what looked like veiled fear and anger hidden under what seemed to be a carefully constructed smile. I inquired what role individual accountability and unconditional love played in his healing methods, rather than the blaming of evil spirits for his parishioner's woes. Needless to say, the pastor and I failed to see eye to eye.

I directed the pastor's attention to his church's doctrine because its position on spirit obsession/possession is clear. In a pamphlet distributed by the National Spiritualist Association of Churches (NSAC) entitled, *One Hundred Questions and Answers on the Philosophy of Spiritualism*, the NSAC says: "If an evil spirit can lead you to do wrong, it is the evil within you yourself which makes it possible." The pamphlet goes on to say, when answering the question how can we best overcome our evil tendencies: "By striving to develop only our best and most constructive desires. Psychoanalyze yourself fearlessly and then face the fact that whatever you are you have made yourself. Emphasize your good points and overcome those that are destructive, secure in the knowledge that: *You are the master of your fate, You are the captain of your soul.*"[6]

Showing the pastor that his church's doctrine indicated the cause and solution for supposed spirit attachment/demonic obsession existed only in the mind of the afflicted did nothing to change his belief in evil spirits inhabiting his parishioners. Nor did it seem to bother him that his idea saying "all people have evil spirits within that need to come out" was in direct contrast to his church's governing body. It was then I wondered whether his "healing mission" was really just a way to compensate for his lack of psychic ability. Did his "talking spirits out of people" skill provide him a sense of purpose or, more importantly, did it enable him to grapple with his own issues by projecting them onto others? This is a very serious point to consider if you endeavor to serve or assist others psychically. You have to ask yourself: Do I have a personal motive? Have I removed the log from my own eye before attempting to assist with the speck in the eye of my neighbor?

The trials and difficulties of life are valuable teaching tools. No matter how we conceive of our issues, we cannot truly heal and grow until we stop running from suffering either by ignoring it, distorting it, or projecting it. Former Buddhist monk and clinical psychologist Jack Kornfield writes in his book *A Lamp in the Darkness:*

> Grief and loss and suffering, even depression and spiritual crisis — the dark nights of the soul — only worsen when we try to ignore or avoid them. The healing journey begins when we face them and learn how to work with them. When we stop fighting against our difficulties and find the strength to meet our demons and difficulties head on, we often find that we emerge stronger and more humble and grounded than we were before. To survive our difficulties is to become initiated into the fraternity of wisdom. The real tragedy is when we refuse to acknowledge and respect our own suffering, and instead spread it unconsciously to others.[7]

Accepting full responsibility for your mind, its contents, its functioning, and its healing is essential for both appreciating and developing benevolent, authentic, psychic perception. When dealing with any form of paranormal sensing it is the wise person who looks upon all of what he or she experiences — especially those *feeling-based* things within the mind — as just information that is neither good nor bad. Cultivating emotional neutrality allows you to transcend the dualistic illusions created by your brain. Once you are comfortable resting your awareness in this neutral place — outside the boundaries of right and wrong, free of anthropomorphized mystical concepts — this state of being becomes the seat of your personal power. The seat from where your mind can navigate safely outside the bounds of space and time, capable of experiencing genuine psychic perception.

5

REDEFINING REALITY

It turns out that the notion of a reality "out there" existing
prior to our observation . . . is not correct in all situations.

ANTON ZEILINGER

When you understand yourself and no longer fear the world within,
you can explore alternative means of cognition, free of dualistic
metaphors and emotional distortion. You will encounter strange coin-
cidences when experimenting with extrasensory perception that will
challenge your notion of reality, forcing you to redefine who you think
you are and what your relationship is with the world around you.

Leo Talamonti, author of *Forbidden Universe* said, "The secret of the
clairvoyant's power may consist in the fact that he or she is able to effect
a momentary form of fusion or collaboration between the conscious
mind and the secret self."[1] This *secret self* is the core you: that which has
nothing to do with the ego personality your conscious mind identifies
with as you. The secret self is the energetic aspect of you that remains
timeless and interconnected with all sentient beings and matter in the
known and unknown universes.

Quantum entanglement says when two particles are created together they will continue to behave as if joined even if you separate them by millions of miles. For example if you take two entangled electrons, separate them and stimulate one of them, the other will instantly respond as if it too is being stimulated. This "spooky action at a distance," as Einstein called it, means that either information can travel infinitely fast or in reality the two electrons are still connected. Following this logic, since everything was entangled at the moment of the big bang, everything is still connected. Time and space, then, are ultimately just illusions that create the appearance of separation. So whether you call it remote viewing or ESP, any kind of anomalous cognition requires two things. First, you must resist your logical left brain's attempt to dismiss or "make sense" out of what you perceive. Second, you must filter the psychic signal (relevant information) from the noise (irrelevant information) within your subconscious if you are to discern objectively verifiable psychic data.

Mind Trip

After several years of practicing meditation and studying psychic phenomena, I closed the book I was reading and decided it was time to sit still and allow the process to unfold without my trying to dissect it intellectually. Thinking this meant walk time, my gray baby schnauzer, Lucy, who had been asleep on the couch next to me hopped down to the floor and looked up at me as if to say, "OK, Dad, let's go!" But instead of going outside, we walked into the bathroom where I collected a piece of my girlfriend's jewelry from the counter before returning to the sofa. With Lucy once again cuddled up next to me, I closed my eyes and began to modify my breathing.

I focused my attention in the middle of my forehead and relaxed. I could feel light tension and some pressure as if my eyes were straining, but on the whole all was well. Inside my mind's eye everything was dark. My breathing deepened until I began to feel like I was lifting off.

I had a strange sense of losing my balance — kind of like when you fall asleep, except I wasn't dozing. The next thing I knew, I thought I saw something. As quickly as it was there, it was gone. With continued concentration, the darkness in my mind's eye turned to gray. Then, in the center of my field of vision, clouds began to swirl past. They were drifting and spinning. Then, for no apparent reason, they flattened back into nothing. Again, my mind's eye was black. Occasionally little lights would twinkle in the darkness. Maybe I would see flashes of color or something similar, yet overall nothing extraordinary appeared.

Suddenly, without warning, my mind's eye erupted into a flurry of activity. My awareness was flooded with images. They appeared in an almost indiscernible flux that moved in and out of focus. Strange visions cycled uncontrollably through my awareness. I was seeing distinct facial features like ears, noses, lips, and even teeth. Next I saw man-made objects: forks, cars, and parts of buildings appeared among swirling shapes, gritty gray clouds, and flashes of color. The remarkable thing was each individual image developed from the former in a completely unpredictable pattern. Then just as suddenly as it had all started, everything faded to black. The show was over. I opened my eyes and was amazed to find that an hour had passed. Wow.

I picked up my girlfriend's necklace with my left hand, closed my eyes, and refocused. The process repeated itself. This time, among the mental chaos an image swirled into focus. It became so clear it motivated me to draw what I saw. Within a few minutes, I had sketched the floor plan of a house, the unique landscaping in the backyard, and a very distinct piece of furniture in the sitting room. When my girlfriend arrived home, I described the contents of my vision. She confirmed I had precisely described her mother's house. There was just one small problem: this house was in the Philippines and I had never been there. We were both amazed. Lucy, however, was not that impressed. She still needed to pee.

In my home library I have a reprinted manuscript titled *A Brief Course in Mediumship: Rosicrucian Viewpoint on Intercommunication between the Physical and Spiritual Worlds.* In this book, the author teaches what to expect when focusing on the third eye. He says: "one will soon begin to see cloud-like formations floating rapidly by, whirling, expanding and closing like spirals."[2]

The author then speculates this kind of seeing is actually seeing into the etheric realms. Since the existence of "etheric realms" cannot readily be proven, I have omitted the next few sentences. In the following paragraph, however, he goes on to further describe clairvoyant vision in a way I found very interesting: "As development progresses, geometrical figures will be noted in process of formation, sometimes vague, sometimes taking tangible shape and form."[3]

He then comments on how students may progress with their psychic studies and continues with his explanation of what you might visually encounter when developing your subjective sight: "The next step is the development of human figure. A hand, a foot or some other part of the human anatomy will gradually emerge from out of the darkness."[4]

I was amazed when I read this. Nearly 100 years ago, this author described his subjective psychic processes exactly as I experienced mine. Could this mean there is, indeed, an etheric reality outside normal sensory awareness accessible through the human mind?

Etheric World or Subconscious

It is exciting to think seeing into an alleged etheric world complete with spiritual occupants is as easy as closing your eyes and noticing strange lights and movement. However, if we consider the work of Andrew Newberg, Eugene D'Aquili, and Vince Rause, authors of *Why God Won't Go Away,* we can see the Rosicrucian's "etheric realm" is really just a mystical description of the inner workings of our subconscious. Newberg writes: "A visual image originates in the electrochemical impulses streaming into the brain along the optic nerve. The first stop for these impulses once they arrive in the cortex is the primary visual area, where they are translated into crude visual elements — a jumble of abstract lines, shapes, and colors."[5]

Each of our five senses has its own primary reception area. The purpose of the primary reception area is to assemble raw sensory data into preliminary perceptions. Once these raw perceptions are developed, they are cycled forward to their corresponding secondary reception areas. Here they are processed further, before they are blended with emotion and memory, and combined with the perceptions of all of your other senses to create your conscious view of reality.

When I first read the words "a jumble of abstract lines, shapes, and colors . . . ," I was excited because they very closely described the ever-changing imagery I see when I focus on my third eye. It occurred to me that since sensory information is subconsciously processed in different areas of the brain, perhaps a person's psychic capability is determined by which subconscious sensory reception area they are most able to consciously perceive.

For example, some individuals are prone to feeling information (clairsentience). Others are more attuned to hearing psychic sounds (clairaudience). Then there are people like me, who are primarily visual (clairvoyant). I reasoned that perhaps a clairaudient hears fragments of sound because she is more capable of consciously registering information through accessing the sound processing area. More visually oriented people like me, then, would be apt to register psychic images because of an ability to access the reception areas that subconsciously process visual data. As a side note, we can also speculate that if people wielding ESP are seeing into subconscious areas of the brain where sensory data is not yet fully formed, this could also explain the emotionally void, often fragmented nature of genuine psychic perceptions.

My next question was whether any proof existed for the ability to see into one's own subconscious. Evidence for such a natural ability is found in a condition called *blindsight*.

Blindsight occurs when damage to the primary visual reception area prevents raw imagery from being forwarded to the secondary visual areas for refinement. With this break in communication, what we "see," never makes it to conscious awareness. The result is blindness.

But blindsight demonstrates some human beings can recognize objects and movement despite being technically blind. Dr. Andrew Newberg describes blindsight in *Why God Won't Go Away:* "The rough visual patterns discerned by the primary visual area can't be perceived by the conscious mind, but there is evidence that the brain can become aware of them on an unconscious level." A few lines later Dr. Newberg goes on to say:

> People who suffer such damage to the primary perception
> area consider themselves totally blind; yet despite their lack of
> conscious sight, they are able to reach out to objects in front of
> them, correctly answer questions about objects they are "looking"
> at and may even make their way through crowded rooms. Their
> "blindsight" is the result of the brain's unconscious ability to
> recognize unformed visual data that, as raw as it may be, is
> apparently informative enough to allow the individuals to safely
> negotiate their physical surroundings.[6]

Now that we know blindsight is simply the brain's ability to register the contents of our subconscious, is it that much of a leap to hypothesize that extrasensory perception is just a similar ability to see into the subconscious where information exists outside the scope of ordinary conscious awareness? This conclusion seems rational given the often impersonal nature of accurate psychic data, such as what one person might discern for another. However, sensing information pertinent to other people would suggest your subconscious contains, or at least has within its reach, a host of information that has nothing to do with you.

If you truly want to understand or experience extrasensory perception, you must be willing to redefine reality as well as the presumed limits of your mind. Now, please do not be alarmed. This is not the part of the book where I suddenly lose my marbles. I am not going to ask you to suspend logic or adopt unsubstantiated metaphysical beliefs. I merely want to point out there is much more going on around you than what your five physical senses tell you is real.

Our individual and collective realities are created by what our brains are capable of and, in some instances, willing to consciously perceive. There is a wealth of information "out there," outside your immediate awareness. There are those things you *cannot* discern because your physical senses can only register a very limited range of energetic frequencies. Then there are those things your senses *do* perceive that your mind ignores.

In a lecture on remote viewing, Dr. Simeon Hein remarked that physiological research indicates our sensory awareness consists of only sixteen bits of information out of roughly forty million bits of data our sense organs collect every second.[7] Michael Talbot, author of *The Holographic Universe,* speaks about reality being well beyond what we can detect with our physical senses. He paraphrases the work of eminent theorist, psychologist, and neurosurgeon Karl Pribram when he says, "Remember that in Pribram's view, reality at large is really a frequency domain, and our brain is a kind of lens that converts these frequencies into the objective world of appearances."[8]

The term *frequency domain* normally describes an aspect of reality consisting of visible light, heat-producing infrared, geomagnetic radiation, X-rays, ultraviolet light, gamma rays, TV, microwave, and radio waves, and quite possibly aspects of reality that are beyond our technological capability to detect. Basically, the frequency domain consists of all the energies that make up material and immaterial existence — whether or not we can see or sense them directly using our limited physical senses. When discussing ESP, the most important thing to consider about the frequency domain is that, according to Michael Talbot, "Pribram believes there may be all kinds of things out there in the frequency domain we are not seeing, things our brains have learned to edit out regularly of our visual reality."[9]

Physicists theorize reality exists on three levels. The first level, the place of physical form and action, is called *material reality*. This narrow range of existence is what your physical senses are calibrated to perceive. It is also the level of reality people cling to when they refuse to acknowledge the possibility of extrasensory perception. *Quantum reality* is a transitional domain where energy morphs into matter. Conceivably this is where your thoughts — as well as every other physical potentiality — exist as primordial energy. Finally there is what science calls *virtual reality,* meaning the level of existence that is the origin of the universe beyond space, time, and all conceptualizations.

For the purpose of examining extrasensory perception it is helpful to correlate the conscious, subconscious, and collective unconscious with material reality, quantum reality, and virtual reality, respectively. I suggest this because the conscious mind deals directly with physical reality. The subconscious consists of the mental and emotional energies that affect, motivate, and conceivably manifest as physical form — similar to quantum reality. The collective unconscious could theoretically mimic virtual reality, an energetic source we experience as an interconnected inner stillness at the center of our being. Viewing reality as interrelated aspects of consciousness, we can see it would not be hard to mentally traverse the universe in ways that are considered physically impossible. You would only have to close your eyes, shift the focus of your awareness, and you could visit any aspect of the material, quantum, or virtual reality. In short, if objective reality is an extension of human consciousness, then this would make all manner of remote sensing possible.

Let's back away from the esoteric for a moment and take a more real-world look at reality itself so we can better understand how psychic perception works. Since most of us only rely on our limited understanding of physical existence to define what is real, we'll start by deconstructing physical reality.

Physical reality is comprised of three basic components: locality, time, and space. Each human body, tree, car, or blade of grass exists solely in the place allotted for it.

Locality refers to the specific spot the object occupies in relation to other objects. *Space* is defined as the area that separates objects from one another. *Time* is a unit of measurement that distinguishes an event at a given location from the rest of eternity.

Human beings appear at individual localities separated by space. Therefore logic rationally dictates that, for an exchange of information to occur, facts must travel between two such beings. For example, if I want to tell you something, I open my mouth and project a sound wave. This sound wave travels through space and then impacts your eardrums, causing little bones in your inner ears to vibrate. These vibrations are then converted into electrochemical impulses and sent to your brain. Extrasensory perception, on the other hand, does not require a physical transmission of information. No wave energy is projected from person A to person B. It is thus difficult for logically minded people using their common understanding of reality to affirm psychic perception as real. However, ESP is not inconsistent with reality. It is instead our common *misinterpretation of reality* that makes ESP seem implausible.

Stepping Out of the Illusion

A few years ago, I taped a television appearance for a major cable network. I live in Hollywood, so that's not all that unusual. But something that had happened three days prior to the shoot really *was* unusual. In fact, it made me realize that what we perceive as real is probably very different from what reality actually *is*.

Three days before filming, I was running on the treadmill at my local gym. I was staring out the window at the traffic coming and going down Hollywood Boulevard. I could see buses and cars filled with tourists of all shapes and sizes. It was a beautiful, bright Southern California day. To top it all off, the woman running next to me was wearing the most amazing perfume. Even with all these distractions it wasn't long before the rhythmic stomping of my sneakers against the treadmill began to fade into the background.

I began imagining myself three days in the future, performing the readings I had been contracted to do for the cable show. In my mind, I was looking out at the audience. The name "Veronica" was echoing through my head, loud and clear. I realized this "Veronica" was the woman I was meant to read for on the day of filming. I scanned my imaginary audience and found Veronica sitting stage left — about four rows from the front row. Now that I knew her name and where she would be sitting, the messages started coming. Before I got too many details, I cut the psychic flow short so my connection would be spontaneous on the day of the actual filming. For the next three days though, the information kept reentering my mind. It did not matter whether I was on the treadmill or at home or in the car — the information kept repeating again and again. I knew that come Monday night, I *had* to talk to Veronica.

The night of the taping was disorganized and chaotic. When I finally walked on stage, however, a wave of confidence passed over me. I knew the work before me was ultimately out of my own hands. I simply had to surrender to the process and allow myself to be a conduit for the future to pass into the present, so to speak. After I took the stage, I briefly introduced myself and explained how I work. I then told the audience that sometimes information presents itself to me in advance. Then, as if taking a cue from some invisible director, I felt a pull inside me that said it was time to begin. I turned to my left, where my precognitive vision had told me Veronica would be sitting. "I need to speak to Veronica," I said. "There is a Veronica here and I need to speak to her."

To my surprise the entire theater fell silent. I had wholeheartedly expected Veronica to stand up the minute I said her name — like some psychic version of *The Price Is Right*. You know the drill, right? "Come on down! You're the next contestant on . . ." and then tears, excitement, and a big nervous smile. That's not what happened. Instead of beginning a spontaneous reading with a woman named Veronica, I was faced with 250 blank faces staring up at me from the studio audience, waiting for me to do something.

The vision I had on the treadmill had not included dead air time. Every second that went by felt like an eternity. To help things along, I added a physical description to the name Veronica, and then gestured to the area where I believed she was sitting. Still, no one responded.

The audience was now getting anxious. The TV cameras were rolling, it was hot, and no one was acknowledging the name or the description I provided. Could I have been mistaken? Maybe there was no Veronica. I started to get nervous, but I tried to remain positive. I had an inner certainty someone would speak up. My confidence began to wane, however, when still another minute passed and no one named Veronica announced herself.

The room was deathly quiet. I swear I could hear a little cricket chirp a sad song from the back of the theatre. Nonetheless, I pushed forward. I again indicated where I thought Veronica was sitting and repeated her name, but still there was no response. Perhaps I really had made a mistake. Maybe there was no Veronica after all. Could I have imagined her? Just when I was about to apologize to the audience, a woman sheepishly raised her hand. She was sitting stage left, four rows from the front. "I'm Veronica," she said. "Do you mean me?"

What a relief. I let out an exaggerated sigh, a big smile, and then shared a good laugh with the audience before getting back to the business at hand.

Over the next few minutes I conveyed details of Veronica's life as they flowed into my psychic awareness. I addressed issues concerning her career, her mother who had passed away, and I described a volatile past relationship with a man with whom she had also lost a child. I was grateful to Veronica for allowing me to share her life for a few moments. It was healing to recognize that, regardless of past grief, we are all loved.

I tell you the story about Veronica not to give an example of a psychic reading, but to reveal how ESP relies upon an underlying aspect of reality, one that is far different from how your brain structures your normal day-to-day experiences. Your brain organizes the "eternal now" into linear segments of time that we call past, present, and future. It reinforces a sense of individuality by affirming our separateness from one another. Yet here I was, able to psychically discern someone's past by predicting a future interaction! Think about it. Three days before filming, I was on a treadmill imagining I was discerning information about someone's past whom I had never met that later turned out to be true. Does this mean that, under the correct conditions, you can bypass the way the brain localizes your awareness, putting you in touch with an omnipresent field of consciousness where the illusions of individuality, time, and space do not exist? My experience says the answer is a resounding yes.

According to systems philosopher and integral theorist Ervin Laszlo:

> The commonsense assumption is that consciousness is a stream of experience produced by the brain. As long as the brain functions, there is consciousness; when the brain shuts down, consciousness vanishes. This, however, is not necessarily the case. It could be that our brain no more produces consciousness than the radio produces the symphony that comes through its speakers. The symphony, too, disappears when the radio is shut down, yet we know that it's not produced by the radio. Both the radio and the brain pick up signals, transform them, and display the result in our stream of conscious experience.[10]

If the brain does not construct consciousness, where does the information come from that creates our experience of conscious reality?

If you want to see the average intellectual roll their eyes as if you are speaking metaphysical hyperbole, tell them the physical world is a kind of macroscopic illusion generated by an underlying microscopic field of coherent energy. This may sound like mystical nonsense but this microscopic field of coherent energy, what I referred to as an omnipresent field of consciousness a few sentences ago, is what some scientists call the *Zero Point Field* or *implicate order.* It is the subtly ordered aspect of existence that is believed could be responsible not only for what we perceive as objective reality but also all manner of occult phenomena.

The only theory that explains most paranormal phenomena and ESP is the notion that information is distributed evenly throughout space within our seemingly objective reality. This may sound implausible yet a growing number of researchers, beginning with Walter Shempp and including Lynne McTaggart, author of *The Field,* believe that "short- and long-term memory doesn't reside in our brain at all, but instead is stored in the Zero Point Field."[11] This theory is called quantum memory. McTaggart goes on to say that Ervin Laszlo would argue, building on Shempp's quantum memory theory, "that the brain is simply the retrieval and read-out mechanism of the ultimate storage medium — The Field."[12]

With Ervin Laszlo hypothesizing that human memory is stored *outside* the brain in a Zero Point Field akin to a ubiquitous external hard drive — and that your brain works like a computer's operating system, retrieving information as needed from this source — we can conceive of extrasensory perception in a whole new way.

If this theory is correct, then any argument against extrasensory perception could be neutralized. I say this because assuming that your physical brain retrieves information stored as energy, quantum memory suggests the ordinary act of recollection is the same as how psychics discern extrasensory information.

Furthermore, if human memory and extrasensory perception use the same retrieval system, the key to understanding ESP changes. No longer are we asking how the psychic's mind operates "differently"; instead, we are looking into how psychics can collect information outside of their own individual memory bank. We will answer this question later when we discuss the concept of "need relevance." For now, the question to ask is whether there could really be such a thing as an external quantum hard drive.

In Judeo-Christian traditions, the Book of Life is said to be a divine record where the deeds of all men are recorded for eternity. In the Hebrew Old Testament, *akasha* is a term that means "cosmic waters." Anyone who recalls the biblical account of creation remembers that the first chapter of Genesis says, "And the earth was without form, and void; And the spirit of God moved upon the face of the waters."[13] Could the ocean mentioned here be "cosmic waters," a sea of energy from which creation sprung rather than a literal salt-water ocean? As *Science Daily* reports, "Scientists believe that a plasma of quarks and gluons existed a few microseconds after the birth of the universe, before cooling and condensing to form the protons and neutrons that make up all the matter around us — from individual atoms to stars, planets, and people."[14] This means all physical matter *was* created from an observable primordial ocean, just as mystics throughout the ages have surmised. Only this ocean was a quark-gluon plasma that behaved like an actual liquid.

Modern metaphysics has borrowed a similar concept of akasha — that of the Akashic records — from the Hindu tradition. The Akashic records are believed to be a vast etheric library containing every detail of the entire universe. In fact, the term *Akashic* comes from the Sanskrit word *akasha,* which means "boundless time and space." More specifically, in ancient Hindu mysticism akasha is a primeval element, a kind of energetic fabric that existed prior to the creation of physical reality. It is upon this fabric that mystics believe all existence has been recorded since the moment of creation.

Whether or not the Akashic records actually exist as a real heavenly place is subject to debate; however, there are three things about the Akashic records I find intriguing. The first thing is their similarity to Jung's theory of the collective unconscious. Both are said to be a reservoir of mankind's accumulated experiences. Second, like the collective unconscious, the Akashic records are — according to famed

American psychic Edgar Cayce—accessible through your subconscious. Third, physics now seems to support the idea of a non-physical universal record of all mankind. I say this because the concept of the Akashic records is similar to a hypothesis developed by neurologist Karl Pribram and physicist David Bohm called the holographic brain theory.

To appreciate how psychic individuals can "remember" information that has nothing to do with them personally by supposedly using the Akashic records, we need to understand how information is theoretically stored at the quantum level of reality. Since Pribram and Bohm's holographic brain theory is similar to the mystical Akashic records, allow me to explain what a hologram is and why it is significant to ESP.

A hologram is a three-dimensional image made of light. What makes holograms unique is that if you could split one into pieces you would find that every shard contains all the information found in the original whole. Pribram and Bohm speculate that our brains are a kind of split-off, second-generation hologram that contains all the information of an original master hologram. In *The Holographic Universe,* Michael Talbot describes Pribram and Bohm's theory this way: "Our brains mathematically construct objective reality by interpreting frequencies that are ultimately projections from another dimension, a deeper order of existence that is beyond both space and time: The brain is a hologram enfolded in a holographic universe."[15]

The deeper order of existence that projects the frequencies our brains use to craft reality is conceivably the virtual domain. Metaphorically speaking, this level of reality is the original hologram from which our brains and all other matter were split. Psychically speaking, this would mean if the human brain is a hologram enfolded in a holographic universe, all information about everything that ever was or will be is already programmed within you, me, the environment, and every aspect of material reality, and thus always within our mental reach. That being said, Akashic records and the Book of Life may simply be clever metaphors Hindu and Hebrew mystics developed thousands of years ago to describe this phenomenon. Conceivably, this encoded data *is* the extrasensory source psychics rely on for their impressions. For this to be true, however, the energetic threads that make up the universe would actually need to contain meaningful bits of information.

Information as Energy

Einstein said, "Energy cannot be created or destroyed, it can only be changed from one form to another." Your words, thoughts, and feelings are basically sound waves and bioelectric impulses — in other words, energy. Have you ever stopped to consider what happens after you generate such energies? Do they radiate from your body and continue to exist outside the present moment?

A couple of years ago, I was in New York City for a business meeting. I had not been to NYC since the early 1990s so I decided to visit the site of the former World Trade Center in order to pay my respects. I knew the subway stop, and figured I'd ask for directions to the site once I got there. When I exited the subway and stepped out onto the street, I felt the most frightening feeling — like I had accidently stepped too close to a ledge. Instead of asking for directions, I turned and walked toward this feeling. With each step an indescribable sense of alarm overtook me. I am actually quite a guarded person and do not generally wear my heart on my sleeve, but by the time I made it to the end of that short block I was not only in tears, I was also standing at Ground Zero.

If you have ever walked into a room after an argument or been to the site of a tragedy, you know there is a very real emotional stain left in the environment. You can literally feel the emotional impact of the past on the present. Emotional energy does not cease to exist once the moment it is expressed passes. Each time you walk into a room and feel the essence of the moments before, you are actually getting a tiny taste for what it feels like to psychically access the Akashic records. With respect to our investigation of psychic perception, the question to ask then is: Can a person really glean factual information from energy stored within the environment?

It is hard to think of any culture that does not possess a mythology or mystical tradition that does not include precognition of some form. In India, they have what is called Hindu or Vedic astrology. This practice of divination is called Jyotish. The word *Jyotish* comes from the Sanskrit root word *jyoti,* which means light. Someone who practices Vedic astrology is someone who, by the strictest definition, is capable of discerning information from light. A skeptic might argue that Jyotish and the idea that information can be gleaned from light is nothing more than the primitive hocus-pocus of an ancient culture. Although advocates of Vedic astrology assert the ancients understood that energy, all the vibrations of our universe, contains information. If this were not true we'd have no life, as existence would be nothing more than a sea of meaningless waves of energy.

Deepak Chopra writes in his book *How to Know God:*

The concept of information embedded in energy isn't totally alien outside astrology. To a physicist information is pervasive throughout nature. The specific frequencies that make infrared light different from ultraviolet, or gamma rays different from radio waves, all form a kind of cosmic code. Human beings tune into this code and use it for our own purposes — it is the information embedded in energy that allows us to build electrical generators, infrared lamps, radio beacons, and so forth. Without that coded information, the universe would be a random vibration, a quantum soup of alphabet letters but no words.[16]

In 2005, Dr. Edgar Mitchell of the Institute of Noetic Sciences gave a talk entitled, "The Quantum Hologram and ESP." In this lecture, Mitchell says that on a subatomic level, all matter — including people — absorb and emit energy. This, he says, has been an established fact of quantum mechanics for over seventy-five years. In the early years of the new millennium, he says, laboratory research by Dr. Walter Shempp and Ernst Binz revealed that these subatomic emissions are "coherent and carry information." He then goes on to stress that "information is just patterns of energy we give meaning to."[17] If all this is true, could psychic perception simply be the assimilation and reconstitution of normally subconscious organic energies into meaningful verifiable patterns? After all, the brain already consciously assimilates visual light and sound waves into meaningful images, language, and ideas, so why not subconsciously in the form of extrasensory perception?

In order to understand the significance of your conscious and subconscious observations of energy (patterns of information we give meaning to), I encourage you to look at yourself and the world around you as a physicist might. Every seemingly solid object, including the chair you may be sitting in, your body, and the car you drive, at the subatomic level are nothing but energy. Every solid object you believe makes up your environment is really just vibrating particles that we can speculate are micro-holograms your brain uses to create a macro-holographic reality. Saying the "real" world is not solid — and that your brain uses the energy of seemingly solid objects to create an illusion of reality — may sound like metaphysical nonsense, but not according to British scientist Earnest Rutherford.

In the early part of the twentieth century, Rutherford discovered that atoms, the basic building blocks of the physical universe, are made up almost entirely of empty space. Even more fascinating than this, however, is that quantum physics teaches us that the atom does not even exist in a single location until someone observes it. This phenomenon is called the *measurement problem.*

Jim Al-Khalili, professor of nuclear physics at the University of Surrey in England, speaks eloquently about the measurement problem in a BBC documentary entitled *Atom: The Illusion of Reality.* In it he says, "An atom only appears in a particular place if you measure it. In other words, an atom is spread out all over the place until a conscious observer decides to look at it. So the act of measurement, or observation, creates the entire universe."[18]

The measurement problem is amazing because it implies that it is our observation of energy that literally creates the physical world. All of what our physical senses tell us is real is actually little more than a virtual world, unconsciously assembled by our collective observation of energy to which we give meaning. And since our bodies are physical matter, then they too must be products of observation. By default then, both our physical bodies and the world in which we live are merely manifestations of an observing extrasensory consciousness.

When deep in thought, have you ever asked yourself: who is this part of me that is watching me think? The part of you that watches you think — the "observer" — is the part of you that is capable of extrasensory awareness. When undertaking psychic development, you must learn to identify with the observer within your mind rather than the thoughts themselves. Once you are identified with this, your higher awareness, you can use it to psychically perceive extrasensory data directly.

To review, the term *extrasensory* means information that is beyond your physical senses. When something is beyond your senses, it theoretically exists as an element of the collective unconscious. For psychic perception to be possible, there must be a way for subconscious information to travel from the impersonal collective unconscious into your personal awareness. Thankfully, there is indeed such a transpersonal doorway, and it plays a vital role in psychic perception. To help you understand how this doorway regulates the flow of information between your conscious and subconscious, imagine your mind is like a computer linked to the Internet.

Downloading information from the collective unconscious through extrasensory perception is similar to a computer downloading content from the Internet. Your computer can download safely because it has security software and a firewall. Similarly, your mind has a built-in security program and firewall that protects your individual awareness from the contents of your subconscious and the collective unconscious. This security-firewall function is called *primary process,* and it repels or converts distressing or otherwise extraneous information into symbols your conscious mind will ignore.

Primary process evaluates incoming data according to something called *need relevance.* By and large, need relevance is not an intellectual appraisal. It is a feeling-based evaluation. Whatever information you feel is significant to your well-being will most likely gain entry into your conscious mind, while less significant data will be suppressed. Understanding need relevance is essential to appreciating extrasensory perception. Moreover, it is the key to accessing the "external memory bank" of other people. Very simply put, since your mind discriminates against extrasensory information based on need relevance, to psychically discern data for clients you must develop the capacity to lovingly care so deeply for your clients that their needs become, and thus *feel,* relevant to your own personal well-being.

People who are "naturally" psychic frequently possess an exaggerated sense of need relevance because in childhood they were often the caretakers of sickly parents, siblings, or grandparents. When a child performs adult-level caretaking responsibilities, this sort of role reversal can instill within the child a sense they must earn their well-being by attending to the needs of others. Under these circumstances, ordinary need relevance can become an acute hypersensitivity. Such sensitive people appear highly intuitive and in all likelihood it is their exaggerated sense of need relevance that predisposes them to genuine psychic ability. To give you an idea of how emotional concern can create a telepathic connection, let me tell you about a strange dream I once had.

A Dream That Was Not a Dream

A few years ago, I went to bed one night and all my phones were off. I never do this, but since my mobile was dead and I rarely use my home line, I figured it was no big deal. Without even considering the possibility of some unforeseen emergency, I plugged my cell phone into its charger and drifted off to sleep. Of course, that particular night my girlfriend fell ill in the early morning hours, so ill, in fact, that it required a trip to the emergency room.

When the pain first started, she called my cell phone and then my home line, only to discover I was unreachable. There I was, nearly fifty miles away, stretched out, with the bed all to myself. My deep peaceful sleep became shallow and restless. The still waters of my mind became choppy. I was filled with a desperate uneasy feeling. The more I tried to resist the unpleasant emotional flavor of my dreams, the less I was able to sleep. I was not quite in a deep sleep, yet I was not awake and alert either. Images of my girlfriend entered my mind's eye in no specific way. Again, I tossed and turned. I was beginning to feel as if I were being blamed for something. I could see her pleading with me, but I could not make out what she was saying. It was obvious she was very upset. It was heartbreaking to see my loved one in pain while I was powerless to help. Then, suddenly, I heard her voice loud and clear.

"Jack!" she shouted.

I sat bolt upright in bed. I was fully awake, my girlfriend's shrill cry for help still echoing in my ears.

Because I spent so few nights in my own bed in those days, I looked around the room, fully expecting to see my sweetheart. But I was alone. For a second, I was dazed and confused. I ran to the window and pulled back the drapes. I fully expected to see my girlfriend standing below my window looking up at me. No one was there. I raced down to the front door, but still, I found no one. An ominous wave of fear passed through me. I dashed back upstairs to my cell phone and turned it on. It seemed like it took forever to boot up. There were nine missed calls and a handful of messages, each one worse than the next. I could hear the pain, panic, and disappointment in her voice at my not being there when she needed me. My stomach was now in knots. Before the messages were complete, I was already dressed, in my car, and on my way. When I caught up with my partner shortly before 7 a.m., she was already on her way home from the emergency room with an armload of prescriptions.

In my receptive dream-state, the deep emotional connection I shared with my girlfriend facilitated a telepathic link enabling me to perceive her distress and literally hear her cry for help. Of course, I am not the only person who has remotely sensed tragedy with someone they loved. Parapsychological material and history books are filled with reports of mothers, husbands, and loved ones whose extrasensory awareness informed them of accidents, lost children, or mortal wounds on distant battlefields. These stories commonly include claims that people somehow knew, sensed, or, in some cases, even *saw* their loved ones the instant they met their fate, sometimes half a world away.

The ability to telepathically perceive information about a loved one in real time may sound preposterous. A mind-to-mind link between people, however, may be quite natural. In his book *Entangled Minds,* Dean Radin details EEG correlation experiments conducted by Dr. Leanna Standish and her colleagues at Bastyr University. According to Radin, Standish selected thirty pairs of individuals. The first of each pair was placed in a functional magnetic resonance (fMRI) scanner while the second person sat in a distant room observing a flickering light. What the researchers found was that while the second person was staring at the flickering light the brain of the first person inside the fMRI became active as if they were viewing the light.[19] This simple experiment seems to demonstrate that human beings really do naturally share a telepathic connection.

Not Your Grandmother's Clairvoyance

Old school metaphysicians traditionally explain psychic reality by comparing ESP to the sending and receiving of radio transmissions. But the problem with this metaphor is it relies on an old-fashioned paradigm where people are separate from one another and the environment. In this metaphor, psychic energy must travel through space from the observed to the observer. I prefer a modern metaphor that more accurately depicts the role need-relevance plays in extrasensory perception — while also demonstrating how information can appear within your mind without having to navigate any distance between the perceiver and the perceived. The metaphor I will use is that of teleportation.

In *Science and the Akashic Field,* Ervin Laszlo reveals that teleportation has been experimentally proven since 1997. That year research demonstrated that, on the quantum level, photons projected as a beam of light can be transported between locations across the globe without physically traveling through space.[20] While explaining the process of teleportation is beyond the scope of this book, suffice it to say that this technology illustrates how a transfer of data is possible between human beings without needing any information to travel through physical space. Laszlo writes:

> While beaming entire objects, not to mention people, is far
> beyond the current realm of possibilities, the equivalent process
> on the human level can be envisaged. . . . We take two persons
> who are emotionally close to each other, let us say Archie and
> Betty, young people deeply in love. We ask a third person, Petra,
> to concentrate on a given thought or image. We then create a
> transpersonal connection between Archie and Petra by having
> them pray or meditate together. If human-level teleportation
> works, at the very instant Archie and Petra enter a meditative
> state, the thought or image Petra has been concentrating on
> vanishes from her mind, and it reappears in the mind of Betty.[21]

Archie's love connection with Betty creates a condition of need-relevance within her regarding Archie — particularly when he creates an intimate transpersonal link with Petra. Subconsciously, Archie's relationship to Petra might be perceived as a threat to the stability of Betty and Archie's romance. Sensing this threat, Betty's need to sustain her connection with Archie enables her to perceive thoughts or images in Petra's mind via her emotional connection to Archie.

I have had numerous extrasensory experiences in my love relationships, above and beyond my girlfriend's early-morning trip to the hospital. I have no doubt whatsoever that when we open ourselves to loving and making the needs of others relevant to our own, not only is it possible to intimately feel another's heart but also to glimpse a subconscious reality where our collective memories of the past, present, and even our future exist as yet-to-be actualized vibrations of extrasensory information woven within the very fabric of the universe.

6

ANATOMY OF
A PSYCHIC

You cannot teach a man anything,
you can only help him find it within himself.

GALILEO

he room was absolutely still. I was sitting alone in front of a computer with my eyes gently closed, peacefully centering myself in
preparation for a controlled experiment designed to test mediumship.
A minute passed and then another, and as my breathing slowed into a
deeply relaxed rhythm both my mind and body became calm. All I had
left to do was wait for that certain inner sensation to occur that lets me
know I am psychically *attuned*.

Understanding psychic *attunement* is essential for developing
psychically. It is also essential for maintaining psychological health
and healthy interpersonal relations both as a psychic and a human
being. Psychic attunement should be understood as the process of
asserting one's individuality — your mental an emotional boundaries — and then softening these boundaries to receive subtle psychic
impressions unrelated to your personal identity. Most importantly,

attunement is neither mastered nor complete until you can gently and most self-assuredly reassert your personal boundaries following psychic service.

Many people who identify as psychic have a very difficult time respecting personal boundaries. This, in part, may explain why sensitive people can be so perceptive, but it is also why psychic people can seem controlling. An inability to respect and assert boundaries is also why some psychics theoretically have difficulty forming long-lasting romantic relationships and why they may be prone to stress-related illnesses.

I know psychics in their twenties to their sixties who complain they cannot turn their abilities off and on. They say they are always "on" and as a result many have an inability to understand others as distinctly separate and unique individuals, particularly when it comes to those who they admire or strongly dislike. Such psychic people cannot seem to appreciate that who *you* are has no bearing on who *they* are.

With respect to discerning extrasensory data, psychic attunement is both a process and a state of being where the psychic harmonizes their mind with, and links to, the source of extrasensory information. When this link is obtained it creates a sensation that defies exact description. The characteristics of psychic attunement will differ mentally, emotionally, and physically from individual to individual. With patience and practice, you will recognize through experience your own unique "knowing" that coincides with the establishment of a psychic link and the perception of extrasensory information.

The mediumship experiment was a series of five two-part tests. First, I had to listen to a short audio file and write down any impressions I received. Then I had to answer a list of multiple choice questions. No problem, I thought. Once properly attuned, I clicked play on the computer and a woman's voice said, "I want to contact Alex."

The vibration of the voice struck my sensitivities like a pebble dropped into a deep well creating ripples of concentric circles on the still waters of my mind. I took a deep breath, exhaled, and focused my attention inward. An image of an African-American teenage boy wearing a football uniform materialized within my awareness. This was Alex. The boy the woman on the recording had asked to connect with.

Alex appeared happy. I had the sense that in life he was well-liked and a good student. I could also see what looked like a sidewalk behind him, but nothing else. After a moment my view of Alex began to expand. First a street appeared and then details about the neighborhood where Alex lived came together like a psychic jigsaw puzzle, creating a backdrop behind him in my mind. Little vignettes of Alex's memories appeared over his right shoulder and under his left foot. I peered closely at these little movies to see what was going on. Just then, a phantom concussion wave slammed into my chest, creating a shock that vibrated my rib cage as it dispersed into the soft tissue of my torso. Instantly, the images in my mind's eye disappeared. Just as quickly as this violent sensation occurred, it vanished. My god, I thought, I had just learned what it feels like to be shot. This boy had been murdered.

Psychically experiencing Alex's gunshot wound took me by surprise. I had never felt an impact that powerful during a reading. It was so intense it disrupted my attunement, momentarily snapping me out of my psychic mode. After a second or two, I reinitiated my mental link and began to write down details of Alex's murder. I then ended the reading and moved to the multiple choice questions about Alex's life.

After completing the section about Alex I moved on to target number two. When I began the multiple choice questions for target two I noticed something strange. I flipped forward to targets three and four. After reviewing all the multiple choice questions, I realized they were designed to progressively seed the test taker's mind with information. Being given advanced information is called *front loading*. Front loading interferes with proper discernment. For example, a typical question in the study read like this:

Alex was:

a. plumber
b. a fireman
c. a student

Since Alex was indeed a high school student, this question was fine. However, the next two target personalities I would be reading about as part of the study were indeed a fireman and a plumber, respectively. This was a problem because after reading the very first question about Alex, my brain was already contaminated with information that would make it more difficult for me to accurately discern the future targets. Since I read the words "firefighter" and "plumber" in the question about Alex, I now had those words fresh in my brain. Therefore, if I received any psychic impressions relating to these trades, I would have no way of knowing whether I was receiving a genuine psychic impression or if my brain was just making an association in response to reading the words "firefighter" and "plumber."

The other potential problem with front loading is the questions could have been intentionally seeding my mind to see if I would accept clues and try to pass them off as psychic data. If the researcher really wanted to test psychic ability under controlled conditions all he had to do was record my impressions and investigate their authenticity, calculate the hits and misses, and then compare them to a control group.

I began to feel like the scientist conducting the study was not being honest regarding his intentions. My enthusiasm quickly turned to suspicion. I do not like being misled. I complained to the scientist and explained my frustration with the format of the questions while he listened patiently. My criticism spawned a polite quarrel, but personally I did not care. All I was asking for was the opportunity to provide extrasensory data without being misdirected or front loaded with potential disinformation. I felt that allowing me to express my work unfettered would yield the best results for him. He did not seem to understand my point of view. Seeing that I was genuinely annoyed, the scientist asked for an example of why I found the multiple choice questions counterproductive.

"Well," I said, "take recording number one for example, the African-American boy who — "

Before I could even communicate my objection he interrupted me.

"How did you know Alex was African-American?" the scientist asked. "There is no reference to the target's ethnicity in the recorded request."

I sidestepped his question and continued my complaint.

"His mother asked to speak with — "

The scientist interrupted me again.

"The woman on the voice recording does not indicate her relationship with the person she wants to connect with. Why would you say she was Alex's mother? Are you sure we are talking about the right test?" the scientist inquired.

This remark felt a bit condescending. After a brief pause to collect myself, I continued speaking.

"I'm talking about test one, section one, the African-American boy who was shot." I probably sounded a little condescending myself at this point. There was a break in the researcher's aloof academic veneer followed by an awkward silence. He simply stared at me with his mouth gaping as if I said something terribly rude.

"How did you know Alex was shot?"

Instead of answering, I proceeded to describe Alex's personality, his age, the fact he was a star football player, and the circumstances surrounding his death.

The scientist now seemed truly perplexed.

"How do you know these things about Alex?" he asked.

I paused before replying, feeling somewhat disheartened.

"I am psychic."

It had taken me a long time to admit that I was psychic. When I finally accepted who and what I was, it became clear you can neither prove or figure out ESP by trying to make it conform to common-sense, linear logic. Even when observing genuine seers, the suspicion of trickery or unconscious collusion between psychics and their subjects is understandable since we cannot go inside the psychic's mind to see and feel what they report sensing. That, however, is exactly what I want to do. As we move forward, my intention is to take you inside the mind — not to credit or discredit anyone. What I am trying to do is show how a psychic's mind evolves differently so he or she can ascertain factual information without relying on the physical senses. I am not saying you should abandon logic or believe everyone who claims a paranormal ability. It is important to keep your feet on the ground in any metaphysical pursuit. People come up with all kinds of exotic ideas to explain extrasensory perception. One such idea is that the structure of the human body is designed as a kind of radio antenna. The logic behind this theory is based on something called the *golden ratio.*

The golden ratio is a proportion that is replicated throughout nature. It can be found in the structure of our DNA and even the shapes of the planets and galaxies that make up our universe. Many works of art, including the *Mona Lisa,* and famous architectural structures such as the Great Pyramid of Giza also contain the golden ratio. The classic example of the golden ratio's representation is the nautilus shell.

For many people the golden ratio indicates a divine order. For some metaphysicians it suggests that the human body is designed to resonate in harmony with the rest of the universe, making the body capable of sending and receiving etheric energy. Although the structure of the physical body may play a role in ESP, I want to instead focus on what could be psychologically unique about psychic people since psychic information is received and processed through the psyche.

Empathy

There are perhaps three kinds of people who identify as psychics. The first is someone who has never had any extraordinary experiences but has learned through practice to access their psychic core and demonstrate credible extrasensory perception. The second kind of psychic is the "natural" psychic who has had paranormal experiences since childhood. These people may also have taken classes or undergone training to focus their skills, yet the justification for their ability is still that they've always been what they report to be.

The third kind of individual who identifies as psychic is generally someone who intellectualizes that they possess ESP despite an inability to demonstrate an objectively verifiable skill. Why would such a person claim to possess psychic perception in the absence of a genuine capability? The answer to this question is that most often these types of people either confuse their imagination and mystical beliefs with actual extrasensory perception, or they distort normal human empathy into a seemingly supernatural ability.

In the last few years, many people have stopped using the term *psychic* in favor of calling themselves *empathic*. But the terms psychic and empathic are not synonymous. *Empathy* is defined as the intellectual identification with, or vicarious experiencing of, the feelings, thoughts, or attitudes of another. While empathy is extremely valuable, it is not extraordinary. Empathy is a common neurological process that creates social cohesion. It arises through the functioning of what are called *mirror neurons*.

Mirror neurons were first discovered in monkeys in the early 1990s and have since been isolated and researched in humans. Mirror neurons enable you to stay emotionally and behaviorally on the same page with others by sensing and evaluating subtle interpersonal cues.

In his book *Social Intelligence,* Daniel Goleman writes, "Mirror neurons make emotions contagious, letting the feelings we witness flow through us, helping us get in synch and follow what's going on. We 'feel' the other in the broadest sense of the word: sensing their sentiments, their movements, their sensations, their emotions as they act inside of us."[1]

For extremely sensitive people, "feeling others as if they are inside of us" is often mistaken for something metaphysically exceptional.

Feeling emotionally connected with others might seem magical, but possessing a highly empathetic disposition alone does not give you the ability to ascertain extrasensory facts. For example, there are lots of wonderfully kind, highly empathetic, sensitive people who have little or no psychic potential. An even more confusing truth is that some hard-hearted, overly sensitive, self-centered people have an uncanny, seemly psychic knowing ability despite having no regard for anyone but themselves.

I am not dismissing the value of kind-hearted people who share the emotional burdens of their fellow man. In truth, many psychics are rightfully very kind, highly empathetic people. Empathy can play an important part during a psychic reading. It can help the psychic attune to their client. Empathy also allows the client to feel heard, understood, and comforted. Just remember, sharing empathetic feelings alone is not a demonstration of psychic ability. True extrasensory perception may begin with empathetic resonance, but it must end with the discernment of objectively verifiable facts learned without the help of the five physical senses.

As we try to understand the anatomy of the psychic mind, we first need to recognize that most mainstream academics do not believe in extrasensory perception. This means when clinicians suggest someone is "psychic," they are most often using the term with their tongue skeptically planted in their cheeks.

From a trained academic perspective, categorizing someone as "psychic" frequently indicates the person in question has a style of relating that includes anticipating the needs of others because they have been sensitized to respond to unspoken emotional cues. While many genuine psychics *do* share this attribute with similarly sensitive non-psychic people, we should not confuse predicting the needs of others with what it means to be genuinely psychic.

Separating the psychic wheat from the chaff might seem harsh, but the hard reality is that there is a clear difference between discerning out-of-context extrasensory facts and knowing how someone feels or whether they need a glass of water. As we move forward examining the psychological influences that predispose people to extrasensory ability, let's remember psychic people and highly sensitive people are similar, but that the true psychic's mind evolves in a dramatically different way — a way that allows him or her to discern factual information via a means that is commonly thought to be impossible.

Black Sheep

A few years ago, I was having a discussion with a well-respected parapsychologist. I wanted to know what he thought made people psychic. I soon found out that, unlike many of his parapsychological colleagues, he was more mainstream in his opinion about ESP. Like I just explained, this gentleman viewed being "psychic" to include a group of behaviors that merely indicated a kind of environmental or emotional hypersensitivity. He did not believe in remote sensing or precognition. He suggested that the acute sensitivity of seemingly "psychic" people was the result of their being conditioned by trauma. I challenged him on this theory because by my estimation there is a difference between being "sensitive" (as he viewed it) and having the ability to discern credible, objectively verifiable extrasensory facts. He stuck to his guns, however, reasserting that trauma was at the root of the "psychically" perceptive personality. I was not sure if I was offended by his hypothesis, but something about his insight made me very curious.

Not long after speaking with my parapsychologist colleague, I began consulting on a murder case that led to an intriguing telephone conversation with an internationally known psychic-medium. I had never met this particular psychic before, so like any strangers who speak for the first time, the first few moments of our conversation were spent politely feeling each other out. Out of the blue, he surprised me by asking a series of personal questions about my family life. He spoke candidly about his own alcoholic father, explaining he was curious about me because he noticed all the psychic people he knew had come from messed up backgrounds. This triggered my memory of the brief conversation I'd had with my parapsychologist associate only weeks before. What a strange coincidence, I thought. Within a month, two well-respected individuals had mentioned the role childhood trauma plays in developing a psychic disposition. Perhaps it was time I give this *conditioning theory* some serious thought.

I began my own investigation into whether childhood conditioning facilitates extrasensory perception. I certainly understood how trauma could make one hypersensitive — the kind of hypersensitivity a therapist might think is akin to being "psychic." For example, author and therapist Wayne Muller writes in his book *Legacy of the Heart:*

> A painful childhood invariably focuses our attention on our
> inner life. In response to childhood hurt, we learn to cultivate
> heightened awareness, and sharpen our capacity to discern
> how things move and change in our environment. Childhood
> pain encourages us to watch things more closely, to listen more
> carefully, to attend to the subtle imbalances that arise within and
> around us. We develop an exquisite ability to feel the feelings of
> others, and we become exceptionally mindful of every conflict,
> every flicker of hope or despair, every piece of information that
> may hold some teaching for us.[2]

Maybe my colleagues were onto something. Emotional sensitivity and a keen inner awareness could easily result from abuse, I surmised; but based on my experience, I knew that sensitivity alone was not psychic. I started asking much deeper questions about the underlying nature of extrasensory perception, comparing my personal experiences with those of other psychics. In particular, I was curious about the inner lives of difficult personalities who profess psychic ability despite an inability to objectively verify their claims.

During my investigation, I could not single out folks whose ability was suspect as that did not seem fair. So I spoke with a variety of reported extrasensory individuals with varying degrees of experience and ability. What I found was intriguing. Even though I asked the same probing question to each psychic, the only aggressive responses I received came from those whose paranormal identity did not seem to be based on an authentic ability.

This came as a shock, though not for reasons you might expect. I thought more of the psychics I spoke with would have been upset about my inquiry into the foundation of their psychic abilities.

Noted researcher Gary E. Schwartz, author of *The Truth about Medium* and director of the Human Energy Systems Laboratory at the University of Arizona, compares psychic mediums to different breeds of cats that have difficulty getting along. He says, "Some mediums are like kittens and easy to work with; others are more like cougars and can be trouble if crossed. Like most cats, mediums tend to be highly sensitive, are often loners, and are affectionate on their own terms."[3]

Schwartz also comments on how resilient psychic mediums can be. He continues his commentary on the unique personality traits of psychics when he writes, "One minute they are purring, the next they are hissing. They can be 'catty' at times and have 'cat-fights' with each other. Sometimes they act like 'scaredy-cats' and other times they are 'scary cats.'" He then compares mediums to a variety of different species of cats and finishes his characterization of psychics by saying, "working with them is an adventure."[4]

Please know I am not trying to disparage anyone. I share Dr. Schwartz's assessment of psychics merely to corroborate what you, and certainly many academics, already know: that dealing with psychics can be difficult because of their "sensitive" personalities. With this in mind and to avoid any conflicts while interviewing psychics about conditioning theory, I was very candid and up front. Everyone I spoke with knew my questions would be very personal. Nevertheless, in response to my queries, it was fascinating to observe how hostile some became — even venomously twisting my words, using them to attack me.

I did not force anyone to answer questions they were not comfortable with. Everyone had the right to refuse, and some did. I confess, however, I was not surprised by who became aggressive. I had expected challenging responses from the individuals with dubious abilities. Their psychic identity seemed to be a carefully crafted armor rather than a service-oriented disposition. But I was shocked at how acrimonious they became, despite their spiritual façade. Paul T. Mason and Randi Kreger write in *Stop Walking on Eggshells,* "Some people with BPD [borderline personality disorder] have an amazing ability to read others and uncover their triggers and vulnerabilities. One clinician jokingly called people with BPD psychic."[5]

I am in no way qualified to diagnose anyone with a psychological disorder. Nor is it my intention to belittle or judge anyone. My investigation into conditioning theory, as an attempt to understand whether childhood trauma can lead to a "psychic" disposition, helped answer two very important questions about supposedly psychic people. The first question answered was: Why are some psychic people so difficult and unpleasant when they are "supposed" to be spiritual? The second was why is it that some people think they are psychic when they have no demonstrable ability? Turning again to Mason and Kreger, we learn:

> Interpersonal sensitivity can best be understood by the non-BP [borderline personality] in terms of the BP's astute ability to identify and use social and nonverbal cues of others. BPs can empathize well with others and often understand and respect how others feel, and they can use these skills to "see through others." It is thought that many adults who were repeatedly physically and/or sexually abused as children developed these "social and emotional antennae" as a survival strategy.[6]

Because the psychic-like traits of borderline personalities can result from childhood trauma, could identifying as psychic, for some people, be a way to rationalize the existence and use of coping mechanisms that are no longer necessary in adulthood? In addition, could "spiritualized, psychic" coping skills be what make some allegedly "psychic" people difficult to be around? In pursuit of these and other questions, I continued speaking with many credentialed colleagues and devoured psychological material that explored defense mechanisms, early childhood development, and the effects abuse and trauma have on children. I found that there may indeed be some kind of link between childhood difficulties and psychic identification. But could this level of sensitivity really trigger actual ESP — the kind that enables you to discern credible, objectively verifiable, extrasensory information?

Whether their ability was suspect or not, another one of the most interesting things I learned about the psychics I interviewed was that nearly all of them described feeling as if they were the black sheep of their families. You may ask, what does feeling like a black sheep have to do with being psychic? The answer is: maybe everything.

Technically, the term *black sheep* describes a child who is used as a scapegoat in dysfunctional homes. In most cases they acted as the emotional pressure release valve for their family. Black sheep are sometimes called incorrigible, crazy, troubled, or worse, but underneath they are not problem children. Black sheep are motivated by the belief that if others could see the conflict and pain around them as they *feel* it, then surely someone would help make the hurt go away. Rather than being loved and nurtured for their insightful, compassionate nature and desire to help, black-sheep kids sometimes become targets for abuse by those who benefit from family dysfunction in ways innocent children cannot understand.

Because of their sensitivity, black sheep are deeply affected by the often covert unrest at home and will literally cry out for change when things get too bad. When such children are very young, this tendency may result in emotional tantrums. Being so young, they are unable to manage the anxieties they absorb from imbalanced caregivers and their dysfunctional environment. As they get older, such children may purposefully call attention to, organize a defense against, or dramatize interpersonal problems in an effort to resolve them. When others are happy to pretend all is well, these kids seek to expose the hurt, lies, and injustices within their families in order to restore harmony.

Many psychic adults report that they did not become black sheep because they thought exposing family pain was the right thing to do. Instead they felt compelled to fight for change because unconsciously internalizing family pain made them feel responsible for making things better. The heartbreak for black-sheep children, however, is that their desire to make things better often only makes their own lives worse.

Black-sheep children can be especially well-behaved yet under-appreciated. On the surface, like little adults, they may appear mature beyond their years — while underneath, they are frequently emotion-ally deprived and often struggle with debilitating, low self-worth. In addition, because their home lives are emotionally and/or physically dangerous, black sheep attempt to stay safe and earn praise by rigidly following rules. Sadly, their rigid adherence to rules only serves to iso-late them from children their own age who feel supported, loved, and thus safe enough to take risks socially and scholastically.

Life is confusing for black sheep. They are wounded by those who are supposed to love them and often feel isolated, misunderstood, and unappreciated despite following rules and trying to help oth-ers. As a result of not feeling safe, black sheep internalize their needs. They become increasingly self-reliant, developing almost impregnable defenses, yet inside they remain tender-hearted.

Despite often being loners, the creative sensitive nature of black sheep kids can be contagious. These children, long before they identify as psy-chic, are often charismatic, highly empathetic, idealistic, and sensitive to the needs of others. Consequently it is easy for them to recruit others to support them in their demands for change, especially other family members who may not have the courage to speak up concerning certain dysfunctions. Sadly, though, when push comes to shove, black-sheep kids are frequently betrayed and abandoned by those who originally rallied around them in support of their causes. In extreme cases they are actually blamed for creating the trouble they are only seeking to help their family resolve. Consequently, it's easy to wonder what this kind of illogical cruelty does to the mind of a child.

A Crack in the Mirror

During childhood, having a loving parent or guardian mirror appropriate emotions, rational problem-solving, and a loving appreciation for who you are is essential for developing a healthy positive self-image. When sensitive children are blamed for dysfunction in abusive homes, where they have only witnessed the abuse, or worse been victims of it, the child's perception of reality becomes distorted. When reality is twisted so that black sheep are made to feel responsible for things that are logically beyond their control, these children learn to perceive themselves at the center of other people's problems and circumstances. This can create an inability to respect boundaries. Such children naturally feel it appropriate to sense and tend to issues that are none of their concern. Initially the irrationality of such states of mind may overwhelm black sheep, causing them to lash out. They may be prone to seemingly self-involved emotional dramatics. Ultimately such children are forced to look inward for protection. Like turtles inside their shells, black sheep children remain locked inside their minds, where they reflect over and over again on their circumstances as they try to make sense out of events that defy logic. Over time, this kind of introspection and self-critique may create the subjective familiarity and mental agility required for true psychic perception. In the future, if these children are metaphysically misinformed and remain emotionally unstable, their tendency toward introspection may also inspire paranormal perception as a way to consciously process subconscious emotional difficulties.

Rationalizing an inability to respect mental, emotional, and social boundaries as a psychic ability can be mentally stabilizing for adult black sheep. In the absence of an objectively verifiable ability, however, the fear and stress associated with maintaining such a false identity can lead to a lot of interpersonal problems. Academics stereotypically character-ize the psychic personality as one that possesses narcissistic, controlling, self-centered, manipulative, and grandiose tendencies paired with an omnipotent sense of self-importance. Admittedly, these words are not flattering. But rather than view these terms as insults, consider these descriptions as clinical observations. This way, like an academician, you can see these words indicate a painful preoccupation with one's own well-being and self-image, rather than purely arrogant conceit. By appreciating terms like "narcissistic" and "manipulative" as a diagnosis rather than an insult, you can also allow compassion to guide you to the conclusion that many extraordinarily sensitive people endured painful lessons in childhood, lessons that spawned unusual ways of protecting and caring for themselves — some of which might predispose them to genuine psychic ability.

Earlier I suggested that the stress that drives sensitive children inward facilitates the kind of deep introspection and mental agility that are required for genuine psychic perception. During psychic development, students practice introspection and strengthen men-tal agility by engaging in guided visualizations. The purpose of visualization is to rehearse being a passive witness to the contents of your mind, allowing the teacher's suggestions to mimic how nonlinear psychic information spontaneously forms within your right-brain awareness.

Since extrasensory information arises independently of active thought, in a process similar to creative imagining, when considering the validity of conditioning theory I looked for ways that mental and emotional trauma in childhood might support this same hyperaware, imaginative, right-brain creative state. Could stress somehow inadvertently nourish the right brain and simultaneously make you emotionally extrasensitive in a way that predisposes psychic capability?

According to psychotherapist David Richo, author of *When the Past Is Present*, "Events in the past that were threatening, abusive, or overwhelming produce lifelong somatic effects such as anxiety, depression, a need for constant vigilance, and so on."[7] The vigilance Dr. Richo speaks of, in many cases is the result of over-stimulating the amygdala. I will talk about the amygdala's potential role in genuine extrasensory perception later, but for now suffice it to say that the amygdala is composed of a pair of almond-shaped nuclei within your brain that help you emotionally define your interpersonal experiences. When children and teens are exposed to long-term stresses like abuse and neglect, the subsequent overstimulation of the amygdala can produce a hypersensitive adult with a subconscious expectation of danger.

A subconscious expectation of danger can be anxiety-provoking. Such apprehensive concern can manifest as a fear and suspicion of new people and experiences, which may inspire hypersensitive people to scrutinize their interpersonal relationships in order to justify their sometimes unreasonable fear and nervousness. The thing about such "psychic" people, however, is they are almost always unaware how they can unconsciously provoke the negative encounters they themselves "predict." In a very real way, people who are constantly on the lookout for threats, first as children and later as adults, sometimes adapt to their hypersensitivity by learning how to predict, prepare themselves for, and hopefully preemptively control dangerous situations. Their tendency to indulge in self-fulfilling prophecy is also just as likely. Either way, when a pattern of seemingly successful predictions based on supposedly intuitive feelings occur, hypersensitive people frequently come to believe they are psychic, despite an inability to demonstrate any form of authentic remote sensing.

It is easy to understand how trauma makes folks emotionally sensitive and why people who have bad things happen to them might reasonably assume bad things will continue to happen to them in the future. But does this make them psychic? It may be true that such hypersensitive people are just great at reading subtle interpersonal cues. But it is also worth considering that perhaps they subconsciously provoke dramas to validate their sensing ability. So the question still remains, can long-term abuse affect the brain in a way that predisposes you to legitimate psychic capability? To help answer this question, I turn again to Dr. Richo's *When the Past Is Present,* where he writes, "In fact, during stress there is a decrease in oxygen to the left hemisphere of the brain, and an increase in the right hemisphere, where our emotions and bodily reactions occur."[8]

With the logic and reasoning centers of your left brain temporarily suppressed during times of stress, your right brain is free to function unhampered by linear thinking. In dysfunctional families, where logic is often distorted and trauma habitually occurs over extended periods of time, the result may be a sustained decrease in reliable left-brain influence. In such cases we can see children become more dependent on their imagination centers to help them cope. A rational person could argue that individuals conditioned by constant stress in this way might be better equipped to negotiate the right-brain processes required for extrasensory perception.

Adult black sheep appear to be excellent candidates for psychic training because of their keen intrapersonal sensitivity. They are acutely observant, hyperperceptive of the emotional lives of others, and even sensitive to fluxes in the electromagnetic environment. We have to remember, however, these talents are not psychic in and of themselves, nor are they a guarantee that one has the aptitude to become proficient in discerning genuine extrasensory information. Moreover, participating in visualizations that facilitate dissociative states during psychic training could exacerbate existing emotional or psychological instability caused by past trauma. All psychic training must thus be undertaken with great care, reverence, and respect for both the limitation and highest potential of your mind. To underscore the risk psychic development poses, I turn to former psychic spy Joseph McMoneagle, who comments on the dangers of extrasensory pursuits in his book *Remote Viewing Secrets:*

> Anything and everything we experience in connection with the paranormal has both minor and major impact on our philosophic and theological belief. It therefore changes our very nature. It alters the way we respond to crises, changes the very foundation of our understanding or belief in how conscientiousness operates, the way we relate to others, how we think about right and wrong.[9]

McMoneagle goes on to comment specifically about psychic development when he writes: "Those who aren't mentally stable at the outset do not possess the critical thinking skills that can protect them from sudden and damaging change. It's only a matter of time before they are irrevocably damaged."[10]

Dealing with the innermost aspects of your psyche can be perplexing and even hazardous. So it's especially important to learn how to differentiate actual psychic information from paranormal perception and the natural noise within your mind. By doing so, you will be better equipped to discern accurate extrasensory data rather than indulging in ghostly dramatics and metaphysical metaphors as a way to rationalize your projections as psychic.

How to Recognize Extrasensory Information

Psychic information travels into your conscious awareness via your subconscious. So regardless of your personal beliefs, all psychic information results either from a dialogue with, or is influenced heavily by, your subconscious. It is important to recognize, however, that there is a difference between discerning the *personal* contents of your subconscious and psychically retrieving *impersonal* data by *accessing* your subconscious. Whether you consider yourself a natural psychic or you deliberately choose to develop your psychic capability, understanding the influence your mind has on psychic impressions will help steer your awareness toward genuine psychic data.

To discern credible psychic information, you must first and foremost learn to recognize any emotional condition that can signify you are not actually attuned psychically with your target or client. Passing judgment or time-traveling in your mind to your personal past in response to your client indicates an emotional trigger has affected attunement, forcing your attention away from the present moment into your personal past. While performing a psychic reading, if you find yourself recollecting issues and circumstances from your past that you then attribute to your client, you may not be discerning psychic information. Let me be clear. All credible discernment occurs in the emotionally objective present. Your emotions should not take you on a ride anywhere else. Properly attuned psychic awareness is omnipresent. This special state of mind is what allows you to experience all information, regardless of where your brain organizes it on a linear timeline. If, however, you allow yourself to indulge your own emotions during psychic service, your attention may stay focused on your personal memories rather than the extrasensory flow available through your subconscious. If you ignore this fact, you put yourself at risk of participating in something novice psychics routinely mistake for genuine extrasensory perception.

Transference is when you unconsciously impose your thoughts, feelings, and desires, especially those from childhood, onto the present. *Projection* is when you take those feelings or ideas and attribute them to someone else. Psychics who feel issues from their personal past, which they then attribute to their clients, are engaged in transference and projection.

Transference and projection are most obvious when novice psychics become emotionally impassioned, causing them to behave like rescuers. When an inexperienced psychic reader feels compelled to rescue you they try to persuade you. They tell you what to do and how to live your life with absolute emotional conviction. The perceived authority of a psychic engaged in this type of behavior can make you want to listen to his or her advice. And, if you are a psychic who engages in rescue behavior, it can feel like you are doing something good. But rescuing might only feel good because you are serving *your* emotional needs and not your clients'.

It can be difficult for some people who identify as psychic to understand how they are serving their emotional needs and not their clients', when engaged in rescue behavior. The problem, I have found, is such "psychics" are accustomed to enmeshed relationships — the kind of relating that leads a psychic to dish out advice based on an inner knowing that suggests, "We are the same, so what feels right to me is right for you."

Enmeshment means exactly what it sounds like. It is a state of being where someone imposes their desires, emotions, or attitudes onto you in such a way that it negates and ignores your individuality. "Natural" psychics seem to especially have problems abiding by mental and emotional boundaries. For them, autonomy might seem unfamiliar and enmeshment with friends and family, normal. Naturally such psychics impose advice on their clients based on what personally feels right to them. They don't realize the "psychic" knowing they think they've had since childhood is actually a symptom of enmeshment and not genuine psychic skill.

The inner knowing that suggests "we are the same, so what feels right to me is right for you," that improperly informed people think means they are psychic, often results from not having personal boundaries respected in childhood. Overbearing, paranormally intrigued parents justify intrusion into their child's personal space by saying they are psychic when this behavior is only about asserting control. What further complicates this scenario is that children who endure this kind of unconscious abuse are often rewarded with a psychic identity of their own. The resulting "special" relationship between "psychic" parent and child erodes individuality fostering the "we are the same, so what feels right to me is right for you" mentality.

For you as a client, it is understandably uncomfortable to think that a psychic could recreate with you the dysfunction their parent perpetrated upon them. However it is important to discuss this because recognizing instances of transference breaks patterns of poor psychic service and also presents powerful opportunities for personal growth. Exposing instances of transference can help you sustain and negotiate healthy boundaries as well as recover and feel your authentic emotions, both of which are vital to your spiritual growth.

Many people interested in psychic ability are not willing to do the spiritual work that nurtures their soul-awareness and ensures compassionate service. Instead they are happy to engage in transference and projection so long as it *feels* like they are getting psychic results. That being said, some clients love the sort of emotional enmeshment that comes from improper psychic service. They may even try to provoke it as a way to satisfy their own emotional needs. As someone who wants to be the best they can be, understand this: when a client and a supposed psychic unconsciously or intentionally indulge in transference by exploring a shared personal issue under the guise of a psychic reading, it can be emotionally cathartic. The client may even express deep gratitude, even if no objectively verifiable extrasensory information is shared. However, since you now know emotional commiseration is not psychic, you have the responsibility to require that any psychic session you participate in be performed properly.

So how can you recognize genuine psychic impressions? Psychic *impressions* are called such because they are inspired by nonphysical causes rather than linear thinking or observable physical events. A psychic impression is typically a combination of feeling and visual sensations, or feeling and hearing, or just a strong "knowing" of a certain something. A single psychic impression is most often a confluence of sensations impressed collectively upon your conscious awareness. Psychic information can also appear in the mind as a single nonphysically inspired sensory impression.

Some people may hear data, while others may see, taste, smell, or feel psychic information. To help you learn to recognize genuine psychic information in your mind, I will primarily focus on two psychic sensations: feeling and seeing. The reason for this is simple. First, clairsentience (psychic feeling) is arguably already practiced in mainstream psychology. Second, since all people see information in their mind when they dream, subjective sight is something everyone can readily relate to.

Clairsentience, meaning a clear feeling, indicates the extrasensory ability to remotely feel the essence of a specific situation or person. The felt essence of a person could include information such as symptoms of disease, injury, and distinct character traits. When I was younger, my clairsentience was very subtle. It offered nonverbal clues that helped me make sense out of vague psychic impressions. As I matured, clairsentience added a depth and specificity to my work that can be profound at times, regardless of my proximity to my target. For example, a couple of months ago I conducted a telephone reading for a woman I had never met. "Margaret" was the pseudonym this client had given me. The only thing I knew about her was that she lived on the East Coast of the United States, yet before we even spoke I knew she'd had a kidney transplant. I was seeing her blood as impure, and I was feeling pain in my lower back where my kidneys are.

Feeling the physical symptoms of others is not a purely mystical phenomenon. In a 2005 article entitled "Somatic Awareness and Empathic Resonance in Psychotherapy," marriage and family therapist Julie Levin describes the clear-feeling issues of others, calling it somatic resonance. She says, "Expanding on the traditional definition of empathy, identification with and understanding of another's situation, feelings, and motives, somatic empathy includes using the felt, bodily sensations within one person as a kind of radar, to pick up the felt experience of another."[11] Levin gives an example of somatic resonance using a colleague's therapy session:

> Annie mentioned in a flat voice that her mother had tried to abort her. After hearing this, Dr. L.'s stomach tightened and she began to feel nauseated. Suspecting that this bodily reaction had something to do with Annie's disowning of her feelings regarding the abortion attempt, Dr. L. asked Annie what she was feeling in her body. After contemplating, Annie said in a surprised voice, I'm not breathing and my stomach hurts. Annie burst into tears and Dr. L.'s stomach relaxed.[12]

Levin is not suggesting somatic awareness is a psychic ability. However, I would argue the difference between what Levin describes and clairsentience is only slight. For example: A therapist might share an identical physical sensation with her patient, one that is an empathetic reaction to a traumatic emotional memory stored in the patient's body. Maybe this memory manifests as a knot in the stomach or tightness across the chest, but the therapist cannot identify what the tightness specifically represents. Clairsentient individuals, on the other hand, can remotely identify a specific physical ailment or precise piece of information concerning another person simply by feeling their own bodies — just like how I identified the kidney issue in my client from nearly three thousand miles away. Perhaps clairsentience is simply a more specific version of somatic resonance?

Clairvoyance, from the French word meaning "clear seeing," is the metaphysical term for psychic vision. Clairvoyant visions can appear suddenly as flash images in your mind's eye, or they can develop more slowly and deliberately by focusing your attention on the physical third-eye area — the spot just above your brow ridge, in the center of your forehead. I'll talk more about the third eye later. For now, so you can better recognize clairvoyant information, think about what it's like to watch a Polaroid picture develop. When you watch the film develop, first you see strange textures. Next there are abstract colors, followed by ill-formed shapes and fragmented lines. Little by little, a recognizable image magically begins to appear. Psychic visions that form within your third eye can sometimes develop the same way. It can take several long minutes for discernible information to appear. With patient observation you may be surprised what imagery appears in your mind's eye when trying to develop your clairvoyance.

Have you ever been talking to someone when, suddenly, a random idea interrupts your thought process? You might stop and wonder: Why the heck did I just think about my Aunt Mary or a beach ball while driving or making love to my partner? This occurs because you are allowing your conscious mind to relax. When your conscious mind relaxes, extraneous subconscious information can intrude into conscious awareness.

Normally our conscious mind is focused on linear tasks and problem solving. It ignores the subconscious so we can get on successfully with day-to-day living. To learn extrasensory perception, however, we must expand our awareness to include subconscious information. In fact, the very first way to recognize extrasensory data from the rest of the "normal" thoughts in your head, is to notice what information seems out of context and inconsistent with linear thinking.

In addition to them being out of context, there are four ways you can discern psychic impressions from normal everyday thinking. They are:

1. the way psychic perceptions enter your conscious awareness
2. what they look like
3. how they feel
4. the fact that they remain fixed over time, rather than waning in significance or subtly changing with each recollection

Psychic impressions enter your consciousness as impersonal bits of data. They can feel like party crashers, bursting into conscious awareness.

Impressions may interject themselves in between — or spontaneously override — conventional thoughts, momentarily stealing your attention. They may appear grouped according to context, but generally they're not sequenced by linear logic the way ordinary thoughts are.

Part of what can make psychic impressions confusing is that while the visual details of an impression may appear incomplete, the boldness and brightness of it *feels* uncharacteristically important. Psychic impressions often look brighter and feel bolder than ordinary thoughts because they carry an emotional flavor or a certain "sense" of something that is not visually apparent.

Yesterday, for instance, I was doing a group reading at the home of two producers looking to develop a television program about my work. I had provided several details that indicated my psychic link was for one of these gentlemen. Then, in my mind's eye, I saw only the arms of a man as he was extending them outward and down. I replicated this motion for my audience. This fragmented piece of information felt urgent to me. I could feel the need to expose my wrist watch from under the cuff of my sleeve. I then said, "I want you to notice my watch. I do not know why but I feel like I want to show off my fancy watch." I did not see a watch face in my mind's eye though. All I saw was the arm movement, the underside of the watch band on a wrist, and the urgent intention to show off "my fancy watch." Had my mind not been trained to recognize the urgent feeling associated with the watch, I would have ignored it and simply replicated the arm motion that surely would have been meaningless. Obviously, the personal sentiment attached to the watch was significant. After I relayed this information, my host smiled coyly because he realized I was connecting with his former partner. He then extended his own arm revealing an expensive watch he had inherited from the man inhabiting my mind's eye.

When I say psychic impressions *feel* different from "regular thoughts," I am not talking about an emotional response. Remember, if you experience an emotional reaction during psychic service there is a high probability the data you are processing is connected to a subconscious, personal issue of your own. When a genuine psychic impression appears in your mind, you should notice a distinct lack of emotion. That said, you may feel a sense of alarm accompanying certain pieces of information — a sense of urgency not unlike the surprise you feel when an instant message pops up on your computer screen.

To get a true sense of what it feels like to perceive psychic data, it's helpful to talk about something called *perceptual sets*. The brain observes the context of your experiences and arranges them into recognizable patterns. By remembering information according to recognizable patterns, you can quickly recall or detect similar information in the future. If I list the numbers 1, 2, 3 . . . 5, your brain will most likely "read" the number "4" even though it is not on the page. This is because you have a perceptual set of the numbers one through five, and it includes four — whether or not the four is there. Psychic perception feels similar. Your subconscious higher awareness automatically completes patterns by whispering information to you.

Pretend the entire universe is represented by a perceptual set of numbers, but that your physical senses only allow you to perceive the even ones. This means the average person walks around experiencing life as 2, 4, 6, 8, 10, and so on. Yet the universe is actually made of all numbers, from one up to infinity. Moreover, at your core you possess an intelligence that can perceive the entire context of the universe. While the conscious mind may only recognize 2, 4, 6, 8, 10 . . . as real, under the right conditions the subconscious is capable of whispering 1, 3, 5, 7, 9, 11 . . . as a psychic impression.

This brings up a question about conscious versus subconscious perception. As I said before, receiving psychic impressions can feel like a surprise. This means there would have to be a part of your mind so separate from "you" that it can sneak up and surprise you. In fact, neuroscientific research indicates there may indeed be an intelligent aspect of your mind that is separate from the "you" that is the thinker of your thoughts.

In her book *Emotional Alchemy,* psychotherapist Tara Bennett-Goleman discusses the work of neurosurgeon Dr. Benjamin Libet. According to Bennett-Goleman, Dr. Libet performed experiments while conducting brain surgery in which he asked his patients to move a finger while he observed their brain activity. Using a clock that recorded time in thousandths of a second, Libet noted the exact moment patients became aware of the *urge* to move their finger. Simultaneously, he monitored the bioelectric activity in the section of the brain that controlled the *movement* of the finger. By observing these two different areas of the brain, Dr. Libet was able to pinpoint the moment brain activity began that resulted in the patient's finger being moved.[13] Bennett-Goleman explains the significance of Libet's experiments:

> In short, it let him separate the moment of *intent* to move, from
> the moment of *awareness* of that intent, from the moment of
> actual *action.* All this allowed the remarkable discovery that the
> part of the brain that regulates movement began its activity a
> quarter of a second *before* people became aware of the intent to
> move the finger. In other words, the brain begins to activate an
> impulse prior to the dawning in our awareness of the intent to
> make that very action.[14]

The fact that your body can initiate action before you are consciously aware of the desire or need to act suggests your subconscious possesses an awareness that can independently "think" and communicate to your physical self. This further suggests that the subconscious is independently sentient, capable of initiating intelligent action before the conscious mind is even aware of a need or intent to act. In this way, your subconscious is privy to more information than "you," is privy to information *before* you, or is not bound by the same laws of time and space your linear-thinking conscious mind is.

A few weeks ago I was crisscrossing town, running errands. It was just a regular day except I kept having this nagging feeling my car was going to be damaged. I had no logical reason to feel this way. Traffic was smooth, it was a nice day, and everything seemed fine. Yet I was convinced I was about to either get into a small fender bender or accidentally hit something that would dent or otherwise damage my car.

When I reached my destination, there was only one available parking spot in sight, which I took. I felt lucky, except that when I got out of my car I noticed someone had wedged a shopping cart into the landscaping next to the parking meter. I felt an intense impulse to move my car. I could not stop envisioning the shopping cart hitting my vehicle. But I was running late, so rather than search for a new parking spot I tried to move the cart and discovered it was stuck. Should I waste time looking for a new parking space, or should I get to my meeting? I kept imagining the shopping cart banging into my car, but it seemed unlikely since I couldn't get the thing to budge. It was not going anywhere. I decided to ignore my gut and get to the meeting on time. Everything was going to be fine, I told myself. This is a nice neighborhood. I am just being overly cautious.

Two hours later, as I walked back to my car, I could see the shopping cart was still right where I left it. Only now there were three teenagers climbing all over it. Then, in what seemed like slow motion, I watched them knock the cart over. There was nothing I could do; I was too far away to stop it. The steel basket flipped toward my car, creasing the door panel and leaving a ten-inch scratch. Why hadn't I listened to my instincts?

Presentiment is defined as a feeling or impression that something is about to happen. That "something" is usually bad. While it may seem exceptional, presentiment is actually a normal part of life. In fact, laboratory research indicates it is a natural extrasensory awareness designed to warn you of danger before a threat actually exists.

Dr. Dean Radin of the Institute of Noetic Sciences conducted a series of double-blind studies on presentiment. His hypothesis was that the autonomic nervous system — the part of us that operates outside conscious awareness — can scan and then respond to the future. To test this thesis, Dr. Radin decided to monitor skin conductance. Skin conductance is your skin's natural ability to conduct bioelectricity. If you become stressed, you perspire. If you perspire, your skin becomes more conductive. Because perspiration is entirely an unconscious process, Dr. Radin theorized, under the correct study conditions increased skin conductance could indicate a reaction to a perceived threat before that threat actually exists or is known to conscious awareness.

Dr. Radin assembled a group of volunteers and carefully monitored each participant's skin conductance before, during, and after viewing a series of randomly generated images displayed at timed intervals. Each image was either distressing or calm. Since presentiment is supposedly the unconscious scanning of the future, skin conductance should spike *before* test subjects actually see an emotionally charged image. Likewise, he theorized, there should be *no* stress response prior to seeing a calm image.

Amazingly, Radin's double-blind study — which included up to forty trials per person, using 127 subjects in the first three trails alone — was replicated in four separate experiments. Each experiment demonstrated there was indeed an increase in skin conductance seconds before viewing shocking scenes of sexuality or violence. As anticipated, there were no stress reactions prior to viewing benign images. Dr. Radin reports in *Entangled Minds* that "the combined odds against chance for these four experiments was 125,000 to 1 in favor of a genuine presentiment effect."[15]

Because of the work done by Dr. Benjamin Libet and Dr. Dean Radin, we now know two very important things. First, the subconscious is capable of initiating an impulse to move the body before we are aware of the intention to move. This suggests there is an aspect of our consciousness that is separate from the conscious, physically oriented "me" we identify as "us." Second, the subconscious also has the ability to scan and emotionally evaluate information from the future — outside the boundaries of linear time, independent of the five physical senses. This means human beings are naturally extrasensory. If your mind naturally has access to an underlying, more implicit aspect of reality that includes awareness of the future, is it so hard to imagine that we could learn — or possibly be conditioned — to *deliberately* tap into this deeper more complete version of existence?

So what part of your mind can subliminally scan the future and unconsciously communicate extrasensory information to you? Metaphysics presumes this activity is performed by an intelligence that is separate from you. It's been conceptualized as spirit guides, angels, and numerous other mystical beings. From the rational perspective, however, the intelligence that is aware of the future is within you and the key to understanding this is your amygdala.

The Amygdala

As you now know, the amygdala is an almond-shaped set of nuclei located deep within the medial temporal lobes of the brain. The amygdala creates the emotional associations that help you file and recall memory. It supplies emotional meaning to your experiences by enabling you to sense the subtle nuances of love, fear, distrust, and friendship in your relationships. The amygdala also scans the future, evaluating the potential pain or pleasure of your circumstances. In this way, your amygdala is the part of your brain that notices and responds to stimuli — the kind of stimuli that Dr. Radin's presentiment experiments were designed around. So is this extrasensory scanning function of the amygdala wholly, or at least partially, responsible for psychic perception? My theory is yes it is.

Your amygdala is like a thermostat that senses the emotional climate of your environment. It heats up and cools down as stress increases and decreases. This is normal. For people who grew up under constant threat, the amygdala can become stuck in the red zone. It's for this reason that children from troubled homes often grow up feeling anxious, emotionally on edge, and hypervigilant.

With the amygdala stuck on red alert, the suppressed left brain cannot as easily cool the right brain with logic. This forces hypervigilant people to perceive potential threats where none may exist. For sensitive people who think they are psychic, this can be problematic. They use biologicially inspired distortions of reality to affirm an imaginary psychic ability rather than trusting what they see and hear. Conceivably, hypersensitive people have more intricately diverse and intense emotional experiences than others. So what do their hyper-alert amygdalas have to do with ESP? I suspect it makes them more capable of sensing feeling-based, intersubjective energetic patterns of information via their right brain.

Five hundred million years ago, our ancestors did not have a brain capable of thinking logically. All they had between their ears were simple brain stems that governed only the most basic bodily functions: blood pressure, respiration, and digestion. As a result, millions upon millions of years ago you and I were not much different than other animals, instinctually focused on procreation, food, and survival. As our biological ancestors evolved, however, their brains developed more sophisticated synaptic tissues that grew in layers over the primitive brain stem.

Two hundred and fifty million years ago, the limbic system formed. The limbic system, also known as the paleomammalian brain, includes (among other structures) the hippocampus and the amygdala. With the evolution of the limbic system, our ancestors developed the ability to feel emotion. For roughly the next fifty million years, the primitive brain stem and the limbic system was all we had for a brain. Night and day the amygdala scanned the environment, becoming more and more sophisticated in its ability to read its surroundings, playing its part in the fight-or-flight response in order to ensure our survival.

Roughly two hundred million years ago, the cerebrum formed over the old primitive brain, giving us the ability to consciously think — rather than merely react instinctually. Suddenly, for the first time, mankind's ancestors were self-aware. They were capable of conceiving of themselves as individuals, separate and perhaps superior to other animals. Over time, decision-making was transferred from the primitive sensing and reacting brain to the self-aware, feel-think-respond brain of the cerebrum. As a result, the "environmental awareness" facilitated by the amygdala and brain stem retired into the depths of the subconscious, taking with it fifty million years' worth of sensing and reacting capabilities. Therefore, in modern times, it's not that the amygdala doesn't still sense information. In fact, it continues to operate just as it did millions of years ago. Only now, it is deep within our subconscious, completely outside of our thinking and reasoning conscious awareness, gathering data in an extrasensory fashion.

The Fight-or-Flight Solution

Perhaps the mental activities many consider mystical and psychic are just very normal functions of your primitive brain, conceptualized as spiritual. To give you an idea how this could be true, consider how eons ago the amygdala and reptilian-like brain stem made it possible for our ancestors to react instantly to danger in order to save their lives. Now think about how slowly our brains work today by comparison. Modern humans must first observe a threat, contemplate its significance, calculate a response, and then send a signal to our muscles to react. This sense-think-respond way of dealing with need-relevant information is glacially slow compared to instinctive reactions. Psychic impressions, in their most primitive need-relevant form, may merely be the way your subconscious has evolved to communicate feeling-based information directly into your conscious awareness when overriding normal thinking is necessary for survival.

The primitive sensing capabilities of the brain stem and limbic system are buried in our subconscious. What they actual sense is arguably concealed from awareness by a confusing menagerie of material desires, random associations, emotional impulses, and self-deluded thoughts fostered by the concerns of modern life. Without a doubt, your primitive brain is always scanning the environment for pain and pleasure just the way it has for millions of years. For those whose childhood stress levels put them in tune with the primitive survival instincts of their "old" brain though, these sensations are often seen as more trustworthy than the world perceived by the "new" brain.

In other words, you have two ways of perceiving information. One is conscious, via the physical senses processed by your new brain. The second is subconscious, via your old brain comprised of the feeling-based awareness of your limbic system and brain stem. How you choose to spiritually conceptualize these mechanisms is your choice. From a certain perspective, all psychic development means is learning to access your subconscious "old" brain without allowing your new thinking brain to distort the information sensed there.

There are five steps to psychic perception. Internally, information must first be sensed, then communicated to awareness, and then *perceived by* conscious awareness. The fourth and fifth steps are to express the information you perceive and to receive feedback. For now, I want to focus on the first three steps, which are subjective and internal.

The first three subjective steps to psychic perception can be seen as a linear equation: A + B = C. We understand step A of this psychic equation. Step A is where we *sense the information* using the amygdala and "old" brain functions. We also understand step C, the *perception of information.* This is the ability to recognize and supply meaning to what our amygdala senses. So what about step B, where extrasensory data is actually *communicated to your awareness?* The amygdala's feeling-based information must travel through the mind somehow, from the point where it is sensed to where it is recognized, after all. To solve this mystery let's turn our attention to a different psychological function, one that demonstrates the possibility of subconscious communication between your mind and your body: the fight-or-flight response.

The fight-or-flight response is a good example of your primitive brain's ability to sense danger and then immediately communicate that message to your body without exercising conscious choice. You sense a threat, sometimes before you even know what that threat may actually be, and your body instantly reacts by preparing to fight or flee from said threat. Might that same subconscious pathway, the passage your primitive brain uses to "speak" fight-or-flight impulses to your body, also be conditioned to channel factual extrasensory information from your subconscious to your conscious awareness? If so, this would explain how psychic perceptions bypass the "thinking" brain. It would also explain how psychic impressions can unexpectedly interrupt normal linear thinking as if from an unknown external source, and why the arrival of extrasensory information can "feel" urgent. Perhaps the sense of urgency is simply the result of the fight-or-flight circuit being used.

Let me be very clear about one thing: living a stress-filled life does not guarantee psychic ability. There are lots of people who have endured trauma or instability who never develop psychic ability. Some may think they are psychic, but the evidence is to the contrary. This truth is obvious, but it does not make conditioning theory wrong. I suspect the lack of credible psychic ability in most people is easily explained. The common response to poverty, abuse, and stress is to focus on one's own misfortune. Adversity makes most people depressed, scared, or angry, which in turn instigates acute self-concern causing victims to feel helpless and possibly even aggressive. Under such conditions, it is common to view others as obstacles, competitors, or at minimum, sources of stress from which they cut themselves off. It is this kind of polarized thinking, defensive posturing, and judging that inhibit extrasensory perception.

When you feel your own survival is tethered to the well-being of others, even under stress, the subconscious continues to scan, looking for ways to improve your own conditions through meeting the needs of others. It is this kind of subtle optimism and desire for cooperation that makes extrasensory perception possible. Based on the theory that stress and trauma sensitize people toward extrasensory awareness, taking into account how psychic impressions differ from ordinary thoughts, and adding the fact that psychic data spontaneously appears in the mind like a sudden warning, the answer to what ESP is seems obvious. Psychic ability is an adaption of the fight-or-flight response. To give you an example of how extrasensory perception may indeed function as an adaptation of the fight-or-flight response, let me tell you about a time a precognitive vision literally saved my life.

The Little Engine That Couldn't

When I was a teenager, I had a little junky car that was completely unreliable. It took forever to reach a decent speed, and the breaks were shot. Every time I parked it I was afraid it would never start again.

One day I was puttering up a winding on-ramp, merging onto a super-wide elevated freeway. I had the pedal to the floor and I was barely doing thirty-five miles per hour. Other than my car issues, it was a fantastic day. The air was clear and the sun was bright — so despite all the honking traffic and swearing drivers behind me, I rolled down the windows to take in the fresh air.

In that moment, I was blinded by a shocking precognitive vision. In my mind's eye, I saw black-and-white images of a semi-truck and its trailer flipping over on their sides and tumbling across the freeway. A wave of adrenaline washed through my body as I felt the fear of being crushed. In the next moment, my eyesight seamlessly adjusted back to normal. Wow, that was weird, I thought. I was a little startled after the vision, but otherwise fine. So I just let out a sigh and turned up the radio.

A few moments later, I checked my rearview mirror. All I could see was a giant truck. It was so close to me that the only part of it I could see was its massive grill. I tried to speed up, but of course my little car did not cooperate.

I moved into the right lane. The truck behind me also moved over to allow an even larger truck to pass. A gigantic semi with tires taller than my car roared alongside me. It was so big and powerful that the vibrations from its massive engine were shaking me from the inside out. I was now boxed in between a retaining wall, the truck behind me, and the huge gray monstrosity looming outside my window. Once again the vision of the truck accident flashed before my eyes. This time I was afraid.

The steady roar of the truck next to me was overwhelming. I tried to speed up but my little engine just could not take it. Every passing second felt as if it was going to be my last. My only hope was to get through the last curve of the ramp and up onto the highway. I knew that once we were on level ground I would be able to escape.

The massive semi and I entered the final turn before the interstate. The bend in the road was so sharp that the truck actually leaned over my car, casting a shadow through my open sun roof. I had to get out of there!

I stomped my gas pedal to the floor, praying for a response. At first, nothing happened. After a few seconds and by some miracle, my little car began to accelerate. Unfortunately the truck next me started speeding up, too. A wave of terror passed through me as I imagined the truck falling over on its side, crushing me. By this time, however, the freeway leveled off and I began to gain more speed. I pushed even harder on the gas one last time. To my surprise, the accelerator cable made a loud *pop*, and my little car took off like a shot, leaving the truck behind.

Out of danger, I could finally relax. I checked my sunglasses in the mirror and adjusted the radio once more as I zoomed along. I had driven only a few hundred yards when I heard a thunderous crash. I looked behind me, only to see that the truck that had been looming over me just seconds before was now rolling and sliding horizontally across the freeway. Its tractor was flipping and rolling independently of its trailer, like some kind of a grizzly decapitation. Had I not heeded my vision and sped away, I would have been crushed under the weight of a capsized eighteen-wheeler.

Throughout this chapter I have deliberately used premonition experiences, where applicable, to illustrate the nature of extrasensory perception because, unlike developed psychic ability, everyone is capable of premonition. It is my hope that by using the information supplied here, you will be better equipped to first recognize — and then understand — precognition when it occurs. Not just so you can realize that extrasensory perception is very real, but also because it might just save your life.

Twenty years ago, on the day of the horrible truck accident, I did not believe in anything psychic. In the moments before the disaster I had been thinking about how beautiful the day was — not about my own demise, auto accidents, or even the freeway conditions. Looking back, I wonder if it was perhaps my relaxed mental state that made it possible for me to receive the warning sent to me by my subconscious. Perhaps you, too, can remember a time in your life when you were relaxed enough to sense something unfortunate was about to happen. Maybe you have even had experiences where you "knew" something specific was about to occur. Or perhaps, like my experience with the shopping cart, you can recall a time when you ignored your instincts only to later wish you had listened to your feelings.

Precognitive experiences suggest there is a mechanism of our mind operating in a way that is beyond what is commonly accepted as real and normal. In essence, your mind *is* paranormal. Whether you believe this or not is irrelevant. Research into presentiment, the amygdala and the fight-or-flight response — in my opinion — offers compelling evidence that extrasensory awareness is not only real but operating at all times just beyond the grasp of our conscious mind.

7

EMOTIONS AND
PSYCHIC ABILITY

What then do you call your soul? What idea have you of it? You cannot
of yourselves, without revelation, admit the existence within you
of anything but a power unknown to you of feeling and thinking.

VOLTAIRE

t's an overstatement to say that all psychics come from troubled
backgrounds. No family is perfect, but surely there are well-adjusted
psychics from happy families whose extrasensory disposition cannot be
attributed to negative conditioning. Nevertheless, it's helpful to examine the conditioning that predisposes some people to *claim* they are
psychic. This aids in understanding why there are those who believe
they possess the inner awareness and sensitivity required for extrasensory perception despite having no ability to actually demonstrate it.

There is no easy answer to why some "psychic" people *believe* they
possess a special sensing ability, when in fact they do not. While everyone is neurologically extrasensory by design, not all people are capable
of deliberate psychic perception. From the rational point of view, the
ability to produce tangible evidence is not the same as espousing mystical philosophy as if channeled from an invisible source that cannot be

verified. Without a doubt, everyone has the potential for precognitive warnings and personally relevant, felt intuitive guidance. But the deliberate act of discerning objectively verifiable extrasensory information may not be any easier for the average person to develop than it is to become a master carpenter or concert violinist.

Each and every one of us has something beautiful and unique to offer the world. We should not allow our emotional judgments to place more value on one skill over another. Thus, a psychic is no more important to his or her community than its plumber. Yes, the work we psychics do is meaningful, but just try using a set of tarot cards or your own clairvoyance to unplug your neighbor's toilet. Each skill has its place.

So why do some claim psychic ability when they have none? The first reason is simple misunderstanding about the definition of *psychic*. There is also the fact that some paranormally intrigued folks have an emotional need to feel mystically special. The subjective nature of seemingly mystical work can afford a sense of accomplishment and self-esteem regardless of tangible results. This is only one of the ways the esoteric can be unconsciously used to mask and avoid many complex personal issues.

Through my work investigating claims of paranormal activity, I have met many interesting people whose identities are based on supposed psychic ability or paranormal expertise. Such people often live in their own worlds, surrounded by equally ill-informed comrades who erroneously corroborate the former's alleged knowledge and imaginary skills. In extreme cases, such supposedly psychic folks recruit their children to validate their theoretical ability, even going so far as to say their kids also possess psychic gifts. This may seem harmless, but upon closer examination we can see that such parents may actually be using their children to admire themselves.

When those certain individuals cannot demonstrate verifiable ESP but insist they are psychic, they often distort reality to conform to their beliefs about themselves. A warped sense of reality can be harmful to the developing mind of a child. Youngsters learn to identify their emotions by observing others. They develop logic by reconciling cause and effect against their understanding of how the world works. A "psychic" parent who does not model emotions and beliefs consistent with observable reality can confuse a child, causing the child to distort reality as well, simply as a way to create the stability the parent should have provided.

The number of paranormally distressed "psychics" I have met in my career, who were told they were psychic as children by their "psychic" parents, is too many to count. Among such psychics, I have yet to meet one who can demonstrate objectively verifiable ability. Instead, their skills manifest as dramatic hypersensitivity. This hypersensitivity often leads them to believe their house is haunted or they are otherwise spiritually afflicted when their spouse or housemates report no ghostly troubles whatsoever.

If you are interested in serious psychic practice, you must become as self-aware as possible. This includes understanding your hidden motivations and processing your suppressed feelings, beliefs, and self-limiting concepts. Otherwise, such shadow material can paranormally distort how you experience both subjective and objective reality. If a person is not emotionally clear, it is very common for him or her to try to use paranormal interest to satisfy a longing for deeper meaning and purpose. This accounts for much of the dramatics associated with hysterical spirit rescues, some energetic clearings, and the kind of supposedly psychic readings that consist of a lot of emotional commiseration and advice giving.

It is also extremely common for highly sensitive, paranormally intrigued people to avoid dealing with their personal issues by hiding under the armor of psychic or paranormal expertise. It might seem that such people think they're better than you, and indeed they may believe this is true. Under closer inspection, such a false sense of superiority often has nothing to do with needing to appear smarter or more accomplished. Instead, superiority based on a psychic persona is often an unconscious attempt to avoid honest human interactions that might inspire real emotion.

Nancy

Recently I was having a conversation with a TV producer named Michael. We had just completed an interview and I was about to leave his office when he inquired if he could trouble me with a few personal questions. I hesitated for a moment, but a flash of embarrassment cut across his face so quickly that I said yes and took a seat across from his desk.

The shift in Michael's demeanor from professional to personal revealed that he was hurting. It turned out he had just ended a very difficult relationship with a woman named Nancy. Michael saw me as the perfect person to offer insight into his situation because his former girlfriend was also a psychic.

Michael's job as a TV producer required a lot of networking. This meant he and Nancy were frequent guests at parties, movie premieres, and other high-profile gatherings. Such appearances were essential for Michael to further his career in entertainment. The problem was that Nancy, although a former fashion model and very likeable, was extremely insecure in crowds of people. When at public dinners or parties she would become withdrawn. Within minutes of arriving at a function, she would feign sickness or demand to leave, saying her "spirit guides" were telling her it was time to go because other people's energies were clashing with hers. How could Michael refute such claims? Over time, Nancy's "guides" caused Michael a lot of problems with his colleagues.

Parties were not the only place where Nancy's psychic senses interfered. In the beginning of their relationship, Michael reported he had been intrigued by Nancy's knowing ability. He soon learned though, that the more he gave into Nancy's psychic demands, the more controlling and unpredictable she became. As a result, Michael's life with

Nancy was like walking a razor's edge. Heeding her supposed gifts constantly limited where they went and who they spent time with. What was most infuriating for Michael was Nancy's refusal to accept responsibility for her behavior because "she was only listening to her guides."

The rigid control Nancy's guides imposed on Michael eventually came to include nearly every decision in their home life: what he wore, where they vacationed, which grocery items they purchased. Every aspect of day-to-day life became a battleground between Michael and the invisible people that always seemed to agree with Nancy. If ever Michael failed to respond to the guides — or if, out of frustration, he made a decision on his own without Nancy — she would get angry, lash out, and then withdraw into a depression.

Eventually, Michael's life consisted of strategizing how to please Nancy and avoid her anger. Even with all the energy he spent making sure she would be happy, nothing was ever good enough. In fact, Michael's efforts to please her only caused Nancy to accuse him of being sneaky and trying to manipulate her. Somehow reality had been completely twisted in Nancy's mind, making Michael the one who was taking advantage and trying to control her.

The room went quiet as the emotion in the air settled around us like a toxic dust cloud. Michael had finished his story and was awaiting my response. After a moment, I described my understanding of his situation and validated the emotions I observed in him. Michael seemed to relax considerably, expressing how grateful he was for my appreciation of his predicament. I offered my insight. The issue, I told him, was not Nancy's psychic ability. The issue was how she conceptualized her anxiety.

Michael confirmed my suspicion that as a young girl Nancy had been betrayed by those who should have loved and protected her. I suggested to Michael that perhaps the emotional closeness he and Nancy shared had triggered painful feelings associated with losing control to someone she loved. I went on to speculate that perhaps when Michael loved and cared for Nancy, his devotion inspired her to unconsciously provoke him into abusing her in ways that would feel more familiar. I went on to explain that in the absence of any impersonal, objectively verifiable data, the voices of Nancy's guides were not proof of legitimate psychic capability.

It was important for Michael to understand that how Nancy treated and reacted to him was not personal. Many people who identify as psychic mistake feelings and somatic sensations generated by repressed trauma as psychic impressions. Since issues associated with childhood pain are often locked outside of conscious awareness, when these issues are triggered in the present their emotional effects can be felt without memories of the actual trauma itself. In this way, unexpected anxieties generated by repressed issues can be misinterpreted as warnings from "guides." This process is exaggerated when someone has low self-esteem, the need to protect themselves by controlling others, or the kind of con- ditioned overactive amygdala that results from growing up in chaos.

A person whose hyperaroused amygdala causes them to expect mistreat- ment can twist any situation to confirm their feelings of being in danger or being unloved. It just so happened for Michael that his career made distorting reality way too easy for Nancy. Surrounded by super wealthy, famous people, Nancy was easily overwhelmed by her sense of inferior- ity. She then projected her sense of being less-than onto others, imagining they looked down on her. Naturally this made Nancy want to escape social situations. The only way to get Michael to take her home without con- sciously owning up to her low self-worth was to unconsciously imagine that her intuitive feelings were communications from invisible guides.

In order to differentiate imagination, fear, and anxiety from authentic psychic impressions and intuitive guidance, you must first understand the proper definition of intuition. Intuition does not always equal psy- chic ability. While there are many definitions for the term *intuition*, those that most closely resemble psychic awareness are, according to *Merriam-Webster:*

1. quick and ready insight
2. the power or faculty of attaining to direct knowledge or cognition without evident rational thought or inference

Both definitions point toward intuition as awareness without thinking. I suspect you can relate to this, as most everyone has an example of feeling like they know something when they have no evidence to back it up. Maybe you can recall a time when you knew someone was lying to you. Perhaps there was a time when you knew you should have turned left but instead you went right — only to end up regretting your decision. That inner knowing is your intuition. Almost everyone confuses personal intuition with psychic ability because we can't explain where our gut-instinct comes from. Without being able to point to a cause, intuitive feelings can seem mystical.

In most cases, intuition in the form of personal guidance is not a psychic ability because you are not extracting independently verifiable information from a seemingly objective extrasensory source. Intuition is merely the combined wisdom of all of your past experiences speaking to you via your feelings — feelings whose source remains mostly outside of conscious awareness. In *Emotional Alchemy,* psychotherapist Tara Bennett-Goleman explains the source of one's intuitive *inner knowing* by tracing it to an unconscious, biological process deep within the brain where the amygdala and hippocampus communicate.

> There are many other centers in the brain that store aspects of our memories of what has happened to us and what we have learned. When we face a decision or grapple with a troubling issue, the brain very quickly draws on all the relevant memories — many of which are stored beyond the reach of awareness — and offers us an answer.
>
> But the answer does not come to us as rational thought: Here's what I should do, and here's why I should do it. Instead, the brain gives us the answer as a sense of what is right or wrong in the situation. In other words, the answer comes in the form of an emotional certainty, not as rational thought.[1]

Your inner sense of intuitive knowing arrives in conscious awareness without your having to think about it. It's simply another way your primitive brain communicates to you when present-day circumstances mimic your past. Metaphysically inclined people may interpret such feelings as "spirit" messages, but these feelings are really just your mind trying to protect you from how you were previously harmed.

Abandoning a psychic identity can leave you feeling defenseless, hollow, and worthless. I have seen grown adults, parents, and grandparents who think they are psychic become vicious and even break down into inconsolable sobs when the illusion of their psychic power is suddenly shattered by logic. For these people, it seems, reality really is too much to bear. If left alone, they normally restore their balance by concluding, once again, that their psychic powers are real. The cycle continues: emotional instability inspires paranormal perception, which in turn causes more emotional instability, which then leads to even more alleged spiritual perceptions. This pattern can go on ad infinitum, until an individual's personal issues are resolved, making an unsubstantiated psychic identity no longer necessary to cope.

Being Psychic versus Feeling Psychic

So far in this chapter we have talked about how your emotional life might influence you to identify as psychic, even when you have little or no credible ability. But what are the emotional qualities that contribute to *genuine* psychic perception?

Many people who identify as psychic fall into the stereotype of the shy, introverted, highly sensitive person. A 1974 study performed by Edward Charlesworth at the University of Houston contradicts this notion. Dr. Charlesworth assembled twenty sets of twins, some identical and some fraternal, in order to study telepathy. The hypothesis was that because of their genetic similarity, the identical twins would be more capable of synchronizing their minds telepathically than the fraternal twins. To Charlesworth's surprise, the fraternal twins outperformed the identical twins. It was later discovered, after the test subjects had completed personality tests, that the best telepathic results occurred when the twins had extroverted rather than introverted personalities.[2] One potential conclusion is that the more withdrawn, socially awkward, or consumed by one's own thoughts an individual is, the less likely he or she is to achieve psychic success.

Spiritualists have long recognized the value of an extroverted disposition when attempting psychic contact with what they call the spirit world. In fact, cultivating an extroverted disposition is one of the metaphysical fundamentals of psychic development. Most do not realize this, but spiritualists teach their students to cultivate an extroverted disposition by dealing with their emotions prior to psychic service. This fact, however, escapes many due to the confusing metaphor used to describe this process.

If you are at all interested in metaphysics, you've no doubt heard the term *raising your vibration*. For those readers unfamiliar with the expression, *raising your vibration* refers to speeding up the rate at which the molecules of your consciousness vibrate. The idea is that spirit people and psychic information exist in a dimension that vibrates at a faster frequency than our own. The theory is that if you want to psychically contact the world of spirit, you have to raise your vibration or speed up your frequency so you can send and receive communication with the faster vibrating spiritual dimension.

When I work, my mind sometimes will indeed process information very quickly, causing me to speak more rapidly than usual. In fact, many psychics and mediums talk faster when in service than in their normal lives. But speaking quickly may not have anything to do with trying to keep up with the supposed higher frequencies of the spirit world. I say this because many highly specific, accurate mediums and psychics are quite relaxed in their delivery. I suspect that when we commune directly with the subconscious, the deluge of subconscious data that flows into the conscious mind may simply result in a faster paced speech until we learn to manage the flow of information within our minds more efficiently. Moreover, speaking quickly, without thinking, prevents psychics from intellectually censoring their right brain during psychic service.

When you strip away the spiritual metaphors surrounding the term, you'll find that raising your vibration is perhaps just a process of deliberately cultivating the emotional energy associated with happy, self-approving feelings. Doing so prior to psychic service allows you to feel safe opening yourself in a more extroverted manner. When you are feeling positive, optimistic, self-assured, and willing to care for others, your thoughts and concerns are not about yourself. It is this kind of joyous, welcoming disposition that invites the inter-subjective closeness that facilitates extrasensory perception. Raising your vibration probably has less to do with making yourself hospitable to spirits than it does with creating an open, emotionally positive disposition conducive to sensing subtle interpersonal cues and extrasensory information.

Despite my sometimes extroverted approach, I can be quite shy. I enjoy my solitude and appreciate calm. As much as I truly love working with clients, sometimes my propensity for privacy interferes with my work. So I want to share a little about how introversion and emotional ambiguity can interfere with psychic perception. Then we'll move on to discuss other ways our feelings can interfere with or otherwise alter information as it flows from the subconscious into conscious awareness.

Buried Treasure

I slid the photograph out of its envelope and without looking at it turned it face down on the table. I pretended not to notice how the man seated across from me twisted uncomfortably in his chair. The confused look on his face told me my not looking at the picture really bothered him. My thoughts turned to his long car ride, the expense of his trip to see me, and the suffering he had endured. I could see he was hurting for reasons that went well beyond the photo. The hope he had pinned on our meeting began to weigh on me. I tried to gently reassure him all was well, but inside my need to take care of him was already becoming a distraction.

Normally, I work completely in private, which generally is not a problem. These days most of my readings are performed over the telephone. It does not matter whether a client is in Australia or across town. I prefer solace so I can fully focus within, without any distractions or subtle clues. In fact, when working on sensitive issues like criminal matters or missing-person cases where a crime may have occurred, I almost always insist on *not* speaking with or meeting the client until after the reading is complete. It's not that I do not care; it's because the loved ones might unwittingly try to influence the outcome of my service. But this gentleman, Jim, had been insistent upon meeting me. After considerable negotiation, and against my better judgment, I had finally agreed to have him present as I attempted to determine what happened to the little girl in the picture — who had gone missing nearly two decades earlier.

When Jim and I finally met, I could see he was a very nice man. He was nervous, but clearly eager to help his best friend solve his daughter's disappearance any way he could. This, as it turns out, included visiting me — a psychic.

Jim and I took a few minutes to talk so that we could both relax. He had some very good questions, which I did my best to answer. Before long, a natural pause came between us. I could feel it was time to begin what we had come together to do.

I walked to the window and closed the blinds. The room was quiet and dim. I took my seat, closed my eyes, and released my breath — allowing my body to relax so that my mind could become still. I placed my palm face down on the reverse side of the photo Jim had brought. This allowed my sensitivities to absorb any feelings I received from the image. I then made a telepathic request to isolate the energetic signature of the personality imprinted within the photo and waited for a reply.

Like dialing a long-distance number, the psychically generated frequency absorbed from the photo was broadcast from my mind, echoing outward until the memories of the soul that was vibrating at that exact same energetic frequency responded. I attuned my subconscious with that of the missing girl. This formed a mental link that made it possible for me to recognize information within her mind as if it were my own. Sadly, the memories I received indicated the girl in the photo had been killed.

I picked up the legal pad next to me and began writing down what I saw in my mind's eye. For the sake of the victim's family, I was grateful the man across from me was a family friend and not the grieving father. I say this because the horror the child endured was more knowledge than any parent should have to bear.

I could see the missing girl had been kept alive for several days after she was taken. It seemed her abductor had not even intended to harm her. In fact, it seemed he did not really think through his crime at all. It was only after he abducted her and had his way with her that he realized he could not let her go. Despite wanting to see her happy, the longer the abductor kept the girl, the more he felt like he was sinking in quicksand. The reality of getting caught if he returned the girl ultimately made the criminal feel like he had no other choice but to end the little girl's life.

When you dissolve your personal boundaries and immerse yourself energetically in a target, it is like nonphysical intercourse. You blend your "energy body" with that of another. This puts you at risk: in much the same way as you expose yourself to physical infection during sexual intimacy, so do you put yourself at risk mentally and emotionally during psychic service. So, although I had originally accessed the mind of the victim in this case, the essence of her attacker, because it was part of her story, was able to permeate my psyche like a parasite.

The longer I stayed psychically attuned with the kidnapper, the more the man's warped mind and perverse sense of affection for his innocent victim filled my awareness. I felt repulsed by his unnatural obsession and disgusted by his adolescent selfishness. Even after killing the girl it seemed all he could think about was how "losing" his victim affected *him*.

Feelings of contempt, anger, and loathing welled up inside me. This murderer deserved to be punished. But because of my strong emotions motivating my desire to see justice done, I could feel my psychic link begin to falter.

Emotions like these — anger and loathing for the horrors that occur during the commission of a crime — are natural, but a psychic cannot indulge these emotions and expect to remain fully effective. Thus, it is important to appreciate that during psychic discernment, there is a correct emotional disposition that facilitates psychic attunement and an incorrect state that obscures extrasensory perception.

Buddhist psychology calls the destructive emotional conditions that prevent us from accurately perceiving reality *obscuring* or *afflictive* mental factors. Buddhist monk and scholar Matthieu Ricard is quoted in Dr. Daniel Goleman's book *Destructive Emotions* as saying, "obscuring emotions impair one's freedom by chaining thoughts in a way that compels us to think, speak, and act in a biased way."[3] Exposing myself to the thoughts, desires, and feelings of a killer certainly inspired me to begin thinking in a biased way! I had absorbed his personal energy into my psyche, and it made me feel like I wanted to mentally and emotionally vomit, if such a thing were possible. My mind contracted in judgment, unexpectedly shutting down the psychic link, returning me to standard cognition.

I took a deep breath and whispered a silent prayer to calm and reconnect with my psychic senses. I continued to breathe deeply until I actually forgot what I was doing. I forgot Jim was even sitting across the table staring at me. Then, these words filled my awareness, soothing me like a soft breeze on a spring day. "Choosing to accept dreadful situations as they present themselves without judging them is not the same as condoning them." That was interesting, I thought. Those words seemed to come from someplace outside of me. Feeling comforted, I tried to reestablish my psychic connection. Unfortunately, I still felt disconnected and fragmented.

As I attempted re-center myself, quick flashes of indistinguishable greenery flickered in my head — random images that seemed tied to feelings of being worthless. A flood of self-doubt washed over me. Internally, I started to struggle with my own identity. Jim just sat there quietly, clueless as to the psychodrama raging in my head. Then I saw it again — it was just a flicker, a flash really — a picture I was barely cognizant of amid the emotional chaos in my mind: sloping green pastures that looked and felt like rural Eastern Europe. Self-doubt created confusion that made me feel like a failure. What if I was wrong? How could I tell Jim he came all this way for nothing? I mentally slammed on the breaks. It occurred to me my biggest problem up until that second was thinking about myself and my judgments. What if none of what I had been thinking or feeling, aside from my initial revulsion to the perpetrator's crimes, had anything to do with me at all?

I withdrew my attention from my anxiety and once again centered my focus on the void in my mind's eye. I slowed my breathing and gradually relaxed my body again. It was time to forget about me and just be. A sense of emptiness filled my mind, eventually blossoming into a kind of gratitude and acceptance I can only describe as a deep spiritual reverence. Without even noticing when it actually occurred, my psychic link was restored and images began flowing into my awareness in rapid succession.

I do not know exactly how to describe what happened next. For a microsecond, I disconnected. It was as though I was in a bright, white, sound-proof room with no awareness of my body at all. I felt like I was floating. I could see I was standing at the bottom of a rolling green field just outside a rural hamlet. I felt like I was nothing, and my life was going nowhere. I was filled with a deep desire to feel like somebody — I needed to matter, I wanted to feel loved and know my life had meaning. My focus softened and I began to fall unconsciously into this subjective reality. My thoughts began to chain together as if dreaming, and when

I reached the precipice of sleep I teetered for moment, almost drifting off into slumber. I pulled myself back from the abyss and opened my eyes. Without saying anything to Jim, I focused my attention on a spot on the carpet about three feet in front of me. It was in that moment I realized all the confusion, the self-doubt, and all the contempt that had been distracting me was not mine. It was the killer's. This is how he felt about himself.

Understanding and detaching from the killer's feelings was like a shot of psychic adrenaline. Suddenly everything made sense. I ceased to identify with the killer's mind. As a result, in a matter of seconds, my clairvoyance resumed at full strength. There, superimposed in front of my eyes, was a small town comprised of gray buildings spread out over a rocky, uneven green landscape.

My attention was drawn to a specific location at the back of a house. In my mind, I walked from the rear of the house to a dirt pen that looked like a covered animal shelter. It was adjacent to a small unkempt vegetable garden. The air was damp and the ground underfoot became increasingly soft the closer I got to the animal pen. Once again, my point of view changed. I was now lying on the ground inside the animal enclosure looking up into the overcast sky. I was within walking distance of my home, yet I knew I would never be there again. From my vantage point I could see the steeple of the nearby church rising up into the air above the rooftops. This is where I had finally come to rest. This was the information Jim had been waiting for.

I have omitted most of the distinguishing facts of this case out of respect and concern for privacy. Suffice it to say, the data that came through was consistent with a known suspect. As wonderful as it was to provide some additional clues and encouragement that the authorities were on the right track, I am even more grateful for the valuable lesson this experience taught me.

Learning to cultivate and maintain a calm mind is essential for extra-sensory success. Sometimes the very application of psychic ability can inspire the kind of turbulent emotions that interfere with psychic perception. Therefore, as a psychic you must develop more than just a calm mind. You must also be mentally nimble enough to remain emotionally detached from whatever surfaces in your mind during service.

Cultivating a mindset of personal insignificance helps me neutralize emotional triggers and maintain complete objectivity during service. I enter this mindset by honoring the fact that I myself, alone, can do nothing. I allow myself to feel the truth: I am but a witness to whatever takes place when I am psychically at my best. Thinking this way arouses a sense of reverence and respect for the process that keeps my ego and any emotional entanglements from directing focus back onto me. From this place of inner stillness, I am naturally separate from the cause-effect, action-reaction aspects of human nature that elicit emotional responses.

It is always important to remember psychic perception is a passive process. You may ask questions, but without an ability to remain still and bear witness to what impresses itself upon the mirror of your mind, success will certainly be limited.

In a previous chapter I introduced you to primary process. I mentioned how primary process regulates the flow of information into conscious awareness. Primary process rejects, accepts, or converts information into symbols based on need relevance. Need relevance, you'll recall, is simply an evaluating function that determines how significant a particular piece of information feels to your overall well-being when it enters your mind.

Because many of our feeling-based needs are subconscious it is not always obvious when, how, or why primary process creates a symbol as it does. Therefore, it's important to take care not to accept everything you see and feel at face value when performing psychic perception. An impromptu counseling session I recently had with a very good friend shed some light on how the primary process distorts information based on feelings.

Gerry

Not long ago, I was speaking to a friend named Gerry concerning a dream he had about his deceased mother. Gerry is a very sensitive guy. He was distressed because, although he and his mom were exceptionally close in life, in his dream they were arguing violently. This left him feeling convinced his mother's spirit was angry with him. Since he had no way to make things right, Gerry was overcome with remorse. By the time he finally caught up with me, Gerry was a shell of the normally easygoing guy I knew.

I generally don't speak with my friends about my work and never accept people I know as clients. But here was a friend who was extremely upset. Maybe Gerry just needed a fresh perspective. As a friend, I decided to do what I could to help.

I was certain that underneath all of Gerry's dream imagery we were really dealing with his own grief at the loss of his mother. I needed my friend to understand that just because his mom appeared in his dream, it did not mean he was being visited by her spirit. In order for me to get this point across, however, I had to be delicate. Dealing with people's spiritual beliefs can be very tricky. In this case, confronting Gerry's understanding about afterlife communication could potentially open up a whole new can of worms. I proceeded cautiously.

Over the next few minutes, Gerry was able to identify his feelings about his mother's death. He was frustrated, angry, and very sad. The big breakthrough came when Gerry finally realized the irrational guilt he felt for his mother's passing. On some level, Gerry believed he should have been able to keep his mom from dying. This was not true, of course, but since he was unable to be at her bedside at the moment she expired, Gerry felt he deserved some blame for her death.

Even after getting in touch with his guilt, I could see something was still troubling my friend. As we continued exploring the feelings that were coming up for him, he had an epiphany. Even though Gerry reported being angry at himself for not saving his mom, he suddenly recognized underneath it all that he was really furious at his mother for leaving him.

Once we uncovered Gerry's resentment toward his mother — and the shame and regret he felt for being angry at her — it was easy for him to understand how his mind was retaliating against him in his dreams. Primary process converts subconscious feelings and ideas into images that are more palatable for your conscious awareness. Since Gerry suppressed the resentment he felt toward his mother — and judged himself as bad for feeling angry at her for abandoning him — his subconscious eventually expressed these feelings in his dreams. Given that Gerry's mother was his archetype for authority; primary process converted his self-contempt into an image of his scolding mother. Thus, the argument Gerry dreamt he had with his mom was really just a way for his subconscious to expose the anger and conflicting self-criticism he felt over losing her.

By and large, primary process generates symbols by associating how information *feels* in comparison to the imagery available within your unique mental database. Sometimes the imagery primary process employs to conceal or convey a certain meaning is not as obvious or as logical as it was in Gerry's case.

When psychically communing with your subconscious, you must be very mindful of primary process — both yours and your client's. What you see as a psychic impression could just be a symbol created by your primary process after discerning a symbol created by your clients' subconscious! In essence, your psychic impression could be a second-generation distortion. Since as a psychic you are dealing with the subconscious, an area of the mind filled with private and potentially distressing information, unless a symbol's meaning is obvious and harmless it is often best to avoid interpreting the mental mystery.

Despite what I just said about the influence of primary process, it is important not to assume everything you sense during a psychic reading is symbolic. Sometimes impressions only appear symbolic because what you see is either out of context or so unfamiliar your conscious mind misinterprets what you perceive — as the next case study shows.

Sometimes What You See Is What You Get

My client Jenna was a fifty-something-year-old woman. I had been addressing her health concerns, when suddenly I discerned a memory of her elder brother. I successfully indicated the nature of their relationship and the fact that he was a member of the clergy. Jenna smiled with pride saying her older brother had indeed been a priest. Psychically, I then began seeing Jenna and her brother playing as children. I could see they had a little white box with a toy alligator inside it. As I told her this, Jenna let out a tickled laugh and an even bigger smile spread across her face. It had been decades since she had thought about how much fun she and her brother had playing together as kids.

I paused to take a drink of water and nearly choked from laughing because right then, as clear as a bell, I could see Jenna's brother running wild and chasing her with the toy alligator in hand. He was pointing it at her as if he was trying to make it bite her hair. I saw Jenna as a little girl running and screaming bloody murder, shrieking the way only little girls can. How cute, I thought. My cheeks were aching from smiling.

As it turns out, my vision was only half correct. When Jenna and I talked further, I was shocked to find Jenna and her brother did not have a *toy* alligator. Instead they had a real, live baby alligator! It had been their pet as they were growing up in Florida. I had seen a little alligator kept in a white shoe box, but why would I assume it was a toy?

Maybe if I had known Jenna grew up in Florida I could have deduced the alligator was real, but I think primary process was the culprit for the distortion. In my personal life, I often dream of alligators when I'm under stress. (Maybe certain stresses trigger a primordial fear of being eaten?) When my subconscious viewed the alligator in my client's past, perhaps my primary process converted the live alligator into a less personally threatening toy alligator in order for me to feel safe perceiving it.

Or perhaps I was subconsciously just trying to make sense out of a vision that seemed illogical. After all, it is not every day you see two children running roughshod with a live alligator. Regardless, my emotional need to feel safe and logical can and did unconsciously change what my mind correctly perceived. Thus, by learning to understand and work with the emotional aspects of your being, you can not only improve the quality of your life but also ensure your psychic impressions will be more literal than metaphorical.

Achieving emotional clarity is beyond the scope of this book. Hundreds of volumes have been written on the subject. Indeed, every religion in the world addresses this issue in its own way. My goal in writing this chapter was merely to scratch the surface of how your emotional life affects extrasensory perception.

Whether you are a client of a psychic or a psychic yourself, the best way to prevent your emotions from contaminating the psychic process is to remain optimistic, 100 percent objective, and openly expectant of positive results. Parties engaged in psychic experimentation need to feel safe sitting within the awareness of one another's feelings. Always remember, great psychics use their sensitivity to be more human. They *embrace* humanity. They easily relax into the feelings and sensations that all sentient beings share. It is from this clear, calm space that genuine psychics can sense and see the beyond.

SEEING
THE INVISIBLE

Vision is the art of seeing what is invisible to others.

JONATHAN SWIFT

I was about fifty miles from my office, attending to clients at a bookstore northeast of Los Angeles. Between the drive and the long day of readings, I was getting very tired. As the sun went down, I was afraid I might fall asleep before my next appointment. I grabbed a protein bar and bottle of water from my briefcase and took a few deep breaths, hoping for enough energy to carry me through to the end of the day. I had just enough time to re-center myself before I heard my next client coming down the hall.

Andrew was a gentle man with a kind disposition and a relaxed way about him. I popped a mint into my mouth to provide a slow release of energizing sugar, and began the session. Within a few minutes the information coming through for Andrew revealed he was a schoolteacher and that there was a particular issue with a student, who was a bit of a bully, teasing him. We moved onto certain family dynamics and then to something very unique indeed.

I relaxed into the process, allowing my sensitivity to scan Andrew's physical body. The viewing screen in my mind's eye lit up as my psychic awareness passed over him, scanning first his head and shoulders, and then his torso. From what I could see, all was normal — until I reached his waist. My clairvoyance jumped channels, tuning me inward, where I began seeing something I had never seen before.

My clairvoyance was giving me the visual experience of passing through a kind of fleshy tunnel. The walls were a glowing pinkish-brown, soft and moist. It was a bit dark too, especially directly in front of me, beyond the reach of what I surmised must have been a surgical light. This was really peculiar. I had to figure out what it was I was sensing.

With all my attention fully focused within, all I could see was human tissue. What I was envisioning very clearly resembled a scoping proce-dure one might see on television. Perhaps I was tapping into the memory of an experience Andrew had in his doctor's office? Who could say? I remember very clearly a claustrophobic feeling as I observed tissue pass-ing by me as my awareness pushed forward, deeper inside Andrew's body.

Medical information often comes through in personal readings since a client's physical condition carries a high degree of emotional relevance to their overall well-being. Nonetheless, I had never seen this type of information before in such a literal way. It was truly amazing. Aside from being really intrigued, I became concerned my client might not feel comfortable discussing what I was seeing.

It had become normal for me to view medical information concern-ing the bodies of my female clients. Women are amazing. They are bold when it comes to matters most guys would rather not discuss. Even though I'm a man, I have gotten used to broaching delicate subjects concerning anatomy with females. But this was the first time I found myself presented with information concerning the private anatomy of a male client. I wasn't sure how he was going take this.

I hemmed and hawed, trying to figure out how I was going to say what I was seeing in my mind's eye. Since the information was still flowing, I stayed silent and observed the impressions in order to buy myself some more time. After a few minutes, however, Andrew finally asked what I was seeing. Without any further hesitation, I confessed, "Well, Andrew, I can see your penis." I went on to explain that my awareness had traveled through his body like a scoping procedure. Thankfully, Andrew didn't show any sign of being uncomfortable. Instead he very kindly asked me to continue.

I took a breath and focused my attention back onto my sensitivities, continuing my exploration into Andrew's abdomen. When my psychic awareness reached the bottom of the urethra I could see the reason for this vision. The tissue within his bladder looked most unusual. I began to feel a dry, irritating sensation in my own body. My hands, lips, and mouth felt parched and chapped. The inside of Andrew's bladder looked like an old catcher's mitt. The tissue was extremely dry, cracking, and even bleeding — like when your hands are overexposed to the freezing cold. Andrew confirmed he had been diagnosed with a rare condition whose symptoms included the bladder becoming dry, like splitting leather. I still think about Andrew after all these years and am tremendously grateful for his grace and kindness. I only wish there had been some way I could have relieved his discomfort.

The Human Energy System

When discussing the ability to see invisible things, we can't leave out the human atmosphere. More specifically, it's important to address the issue of whether or not chakras are real — and what role they may or may not play in extrasensory perception.

The word *chakra* is Sanskrit for "wheel." There are believed to be seven main chakras, located along the midline of the human body corresponding with the endocrine system. Metaphysics teaches that each chakra is like a whirlpool of light, sucking life-giving energy called *prana* into your body. Once absorbed into the endocrine system, it is believed prana is converted into the neurotransmitters that regulate and sustain your body's vital systems.

Whether this is true or merely a metaphor for our interdependent relationship with the physical environment is not important. What *is* important, psychically speaking, is the metaphysical theory that controlling your chakras enables psychic perception, and the question of whether your third-eye chakra is more than just a metaphor. I personally believe chakras are real, on the quantum level of reality, although I have no evidence to support this belief. For argument's sake, however, let's agree that chakras do exist. This will help dispel a common misunderstanding about them with respect to their assumed relationship with extrasensory perception.

Every exploration into psychic development I have ever encountered, be it in a class, lecture, or a book, includes a discussion on the human energy system. Students are usually taught that each psychic session should begin with the psychic surrounding him or herself with protective energy. Then, psychics open their chakras, one by one, in order to activate their psychic senses. This is simply a false idea. You cannot open and close your chakras of your own conscious volition. If you had this capability, you would essentially have the ability to deliberately end your own life. You see, as conduits of life-giving energy, your chakras are theoretically always open. If they were closed, you would die.

When a psychic development teacher instructs a student to open their chakras in preparation for psychic sensing, what they are *really* doing is assisting the student in shifting his or her awareness from left-brain linear thinking into right-brain imagination. Envisioning the chakras helps to do this. When it is time to end psychic service, students are taught to return to normal thinking by envisioning their chakras closing down.

In my experience, working with chakras has no bearing whatsoever on whether you can or cannot demonstrate genuine extrasensory perception.

So rather than focusing on the mystical properties of chakras, I want to share a more rational interpretation of them — one that may indeed aid you in developing both your character and extrasensory perception.

In the book *How to Know God,* Deepak Chopra asserts: "Holy visions and revelations aren't random. They fall into seven definite events taking place inside the brain. These responses are much more basic than your beliefs, but they give rise to beliefs. They bridge from our world to an invisible domain where matter dissolves and spirit emerges."[1]

I find Dr. Chopra's statement intriguing. He calls the seven events "brain responses," writing that each of these seven brain responses are "avenues to attain some aspect of God."[2] It is also interesting that there are seven brain responses to experience an aspect of God, and there are seven chakras. With this correlation in mind, regardless of whether chakras are actually real, I suggest your chakras are probably best looked at as metaphorical tools to better know and address those psychospiritual issues that keep you from experiencing a more transcendent state of mind — the state of mind that fosters the kind of extroverted disposition required for psychic success.

Dr. Chopra's seven brain responses are the fight-or-flight response, the reactive response, the restful-awareness response, the intuitive response, the creative response, the visionary response, and the sacred response.[3]

If you know anything about the chakras, you probably have recognized that the fight-or-flight response corresponds with your root chakra where issues concerning financial, emotional, and physical security are dealt with. By honoring your needs and protecting yourself, you are taking care of the first psychospiritual aspect that will enable you to fully express who and what you are.

The second chakra is the sacral. Here we work with the reactive response. It requires you to honor your individuality by creating and affirming healthy boundaries while also appreciating that your value is innate, meaning your worth does not come from what you do or what you have.

Working with the restful response via the solar plexus chakra enables you to realize you can remain calm amid chaos without letting go of your power. Here is where you can learn to absorb and transform all forms of emotion, using the unpredictability of life to empower you. The inner stillness afforded you by your restful response instills confidence so you no longer feel victim to circumstances.

The next chakra to consider on your way to psychic success is the heart chakra. This is the home of the intuitive response. Here you will endeavor to give love and kindness to yourself and others by cultivating and sharing tolerance, forgiveness, and compassion. Without tackling the issues associated with the first four chakras, your throat chakra and its corresponding creative response will indeed be a challenge. Working with your throat chakra brings fearless expression of your authentic self because you know you are worth being seen and heard.

The visionary response is next. Here you will open your third eye. Honor all that you are and how far you've come. At this stage, compassion teaches you when to speak and when to hold your tongue. Above all you are service-minded, sharing your foresight and wisdom without expecting to receive anything in return. And finally, the sacred response is activated when self-realization causes the crown chakra to blossom, allowing you to experience unity with all beings.

Reflecting on my interpretation of the chakras based on Dr. Chopra's brain responses, we can see that I have barely scratched the surface. Entire books have been written about the chakras. The areas of personal development I have associated with each brain response and chakra could themselves be subjects to fill entire volumes. I am merely trying to point out the real work behind serious personal and psychic development. Indeed, you can successfully demonstrate psychic ability without addressing or mastering any of the issues I have outlined using the seven responses. However, without looking after yourself by addressing the concerns associated with each chakra, you may pay a price. So I offer this information here because investing in your personal and spiritual development will keep you mentally and emotionally healthy while you experiment with extrasensory perception.

Just remember, there is no such thing as overnight psychic success. If you have the aptitude and willingness to commit to safe, progressive, personal development, your third eye may astound you for years to come without concern.

Your Memory, My Mind

I reached into a velvet sack and withdrew a nondescript ring. I was standing in front of an audience of about a hundred people, demonstrating a skill called *psychometry*. Psychometry is the ability to discern information from energy that is theoretically stored in an object. It is believed that metallic objects are the best source of psychic energy because of their capacity to conduct electricity.

After selecting the ring, I cupped it in the center of my left hand, while focusing on my breathing for several moments. Little by little, the energy radiating from the ring impressed itself upon my sensitivities. I closed my eyes and stared directly into the center of my forehead. At first I could feel a strain on my eyes and tension in the muscles just above my brow. But as I breathed and slowly relaxed, pictures gradually began to form within my mind. Soon, I could hear children laughing and playing. When I opened my eyes I was witnessing a child's outdoor birthday party superimposed between me and my audience.

I carefully described the psychic impression playing out before me. I was stepping, moving, and turning my head as if I was actually standing in the memory of the ring's owner. I could see I was in a public park. There was a lake. I saw streamers and balloons hanging from trees, kids eating ice cream, and lots of laughter. What attracted my attention the most was a 1940s-era pickup truck parked on the grass — complete with wood-plank side rails over its bed and rounded headlights snuggled within curvy front fenders. I could also see what looked like a kind of push-button ignition on the dashboard inside the driver's compartment.

After I spent a few moments describing the truck in explicit detail, the energy enabling the reading slowly subsided and a gentleman in the audience stood with a big smile on his face. He expressed his appreciation for my demonstration saying how impressed he was with the details of the park he played in as a boy and, more importantly, of his family's truck. When I reached through the crowd to return the man's ring, his face tightened. "That's not my ring," he said. We were both surprised. I took the trinket back from him not quite knowing what to say. What I had envisioned was so vivid. It had to be real, I reasoned. But surely the man who thought I described his childhood knows what his own jewelry looks like! Could I have imagined the birthday party? An awkward silence fell over the audience.

A few women seated nearby checked to see if the ring belonged to them. There were no takers. Other attendees here and there also asked to see the ring, but still no one identified it as theirs. So there I was, encircled by an audience with a ring no one recognized, proposing a psychic vision no one could validate. Without someone confirming the details of my reading, I had to concede that maybe, despite how real my clairvoyance seemed, I had made a mistake. Not wanting to make my situation worse, I kept my mouth shut — hoping an additional clue would pop into my head, one that would reveal the ring's true owner.

From across the room, an elderly woman asked if she could see the ring. I walked toward her. To my delight, as I strode closer, she began laughing out loud, shaking her head in the affirmative. She was the *mother* of the gentleman who originally thought I'd discerned his childhood birthday party.

"I knew that truck sounded too familiar!" she giggled in a gruff whiskey voice. We laughed together as she slid her ring back on her wrinkled finger. Her son had not recognized his own mother's ring. In the end, it was amazing to have this vision independently verified by both mother and son.

As I've mentioned before, the way I sometimes access clairvoyent information is by looking inward at my third eye. The third eye is theoretically located between the eyes, just slightly above the brow line in the middle of your forehead. It is universally accepted as the seat of psychic sight by metaphysical practitioners. As you no doubt recognize by now, I view metaphysical beliefs as more metaphorical than literal. So I must ask whether there might be some biological form or function that led to the creation of the "third eye" metaphor. Since the third eye corresponds directly to the sixth chakra, it is useful to examine the relationship this chakra is said to have with its supposed corresponding endocrine gland. Might this gland play a role in clairvoyance?

I am not the first to speak of a correlation between the third eye and the endocrine system. However, many modern psychic development instructors mistakenly teach that the pituitary gland receives the life-sustaining prana that flows into the third-eye chakra. This is a mistake because if the chakra system is real and it does draw prana into the endocrine system, the pituitary gland's biological function could not rationally support clairvoyant ability.

The pituitary is the master gland the brain uses to communicate to all the other glands in the body. From a rational perspective, it would make more sense to imagine the pituitary gland is associated with the crown chakra, which is believed to be responsible for the human link with the divine. Since most people look at god as the boss — and the pituitary gland is the boss of the other endocrine glands — to me it makes more sense that the pituitary gland would be connected to the crown chakra. But if the pituitary gland has nothing to do with the third eye, then which endocrine gland could be associated with the clairvoyance?

Centuries ago, Hindu mystics theorized that prana flows through the third-eye chakra into the pineal gland. The pineal gland is a tiny, reddish-brown, pinecone-shaped organ about the size of a grain of rice. It is located behind the forehead, between the brain's two hemispheres. The location of the pineal gland is intriguing because it is aligned with the location of the third-eye chakra. Even more interesting than its location, perhaps, are the chemicals it secretes.

The pineal gland dispenses the hormone melatonin. Among many other things, melatonin governs our sleep-wake cycle. The pineal gland also produces serotonin, which regulates such things as mood, appetite, and sexuality. From a paranormal perspective, however, what is most interesting about the pineal gland is that it also secretes dimethyltryptamine (DMT).

According to Dr. Rick Strassman, author of *DMT: The Spirit Molecule,* DMT is a chemical cousin of serotonin. It also happens to be a naturally occurring psychedelic. Strassman writes that DMT "provides our consciousness access to the most amazing and unexpected visions, thoughts, and feelings. It throws open the door to worlds beyond our imagination."[4]

Could clairvoyance be possible because of a brain-produced psychedelic that enables you to experience paranormal visions? According to Dr. Strassman, people who have experimented with DMT have reported out-of-body travel, the capability to predict the future, the ability to find lost objects, contact with the dead, and an array of visual and sensory phenomena that mimic near-death experiences — including contact with non-human intelligence.[5] Admittedly, you can have wacky experiences if you play with your brain chemistry. Even so, how would chemically unhinging your mind from its linear thinking allow you to find lost objects or predict future events? After all, these are not completely subjective experiences. Predicting the future and finding lost objects requires independent, objective confirmation of your perceptions. This suggests that when the mind is unhinged from the confines of physical reality and ordinary everyday thinking some aspect of awareness can access information in a way commonly thought to be unreal and impossible.

For centuries, indigenous people have used natural mind-altering substances such as peyote and mescaline in their spiritual rituals. Similarly, modern science has discovered psychic-like results when experimenting with synthetic hallucinogens such as LSD and MDMA. In *The Holographic Universe,* Michael Talbot references the work of Stanislav Grof, former chief of psychiatric research at the Maryland Psychiatric Research Center and assistant professor of psychiatry at the Johns Hopkins School of Medicine.

Dr. Grof noticed that LSD research subjects appeared to have a way of accessing information beyond what was considered normal. Talbot recounts Grof's recollection of his patients' experiences:

> Patients were also able to tap into the consciousness of their
> relatives and ancestors. One woman experienced what it was like
> to be her mother at the age of three and accurately described
> a frightening event that had befallen her mother at the time.
> The woman also gave a precise description of the house her
> mother had lived in as well as the white pinafore she had been
> wearing — all details her mother later confirmed and admitted
> she had never talked about before. Other patients gave equally
> accurate descriptions of events that had befallen ancestors who
> had lived decades and even centuries before.[6]

Although DMT contributes to a variety of paranormal experiences associated with clairvoyance, this is not the only reason some consider the pineal gland to be the real-life third eye. Despite being buried in your mid-brain, the pineal gland is light-sensitive. Why would this be so? As it turns out, over millions of years of evolution, the pineal gland has maintained a neural connection to the retina. The gland itself is partially made up of photoreceptive cells called pinealocytes, which are similar to the photoreceptor cells in your eyes. According to evolution-ary biologists, this means the pineal gland in the middle of your head could indeed share an evolutionary ancestor with the retinal cells in your eyes.

Not everyone agrees that human beings evolved from less physically complex creatures like amphibians. However, there is evidence of a third eye in the animal kingdom that is hard to ignore. Lizards, snakes, frogs, and certain species of fish like tuna, some sharks, and lampreys all have what biologist call a parietal eye, also known as the parietal organ or third eye, located between and a little above the eyes. The parietal eye is not an actual blinking eye as you might imagine, but merely a photosensitive area. It detects light through a biochemical process rather than relying on rod and cone cells as normal eyes do. What if, as human beings evolved from amphibious origins over millions of years, the light-sensitive tissue of the parietal eye was swallowed by our emerging cerebrum — along with the brain stem and amygdala? With this in mind, could the pineal gland be a descendent of a parietal third eye, buried deep within the brain yet somehow still subconsciously perceptive? Maybe the pineal gland is a lot like the amygdala in that it is subconsciously capable of perceiving and then "whispering" information to your conscious mind.

The parietal organs in animals are not recognized as extrasensory, but their uniqueness and similarity to the human pineal gland might provide clues to our evolutionary past. Can we say for certain that human beings have a supernatural third eye as mystics define it? No. But when the pineal gland unhinges the mind through its emission of DMT, maybe it enables psychics to naturally perceive paranormal visions by sensing information encoded within light. When this information is reconstituted visually and can be objectively verified as accurate, perhaps we can surmise that yes, indeed, the pineal gland does offer some internal means of extrasensory perception — one that suggests that we do have at third eye after all.

Clairvoyance

A few years ago, I participated in an investigation of a ten-acre estate in Sun Valley, California. The owner of the home (we will call her Hillary) complained of a variety of haunting phenomena, including strange noises and odd feelings of being watched. By this time, I had become so accustomed to paranormal claims that Hillary's sounded mundane. Yet I confess, I had no idea what we were in for. If someone had told me what I am about to share, I would have thought they were nuts. Looking back, I suppose it was good I visited that compound completely ignorant as to what was really going on. Otherwise I might have prejudged the situation, making it impossible to have the experience I did.

The investigation began with my colleague Richard interviewing Hillary and taking electromagnetic measurements while I toured the grounds with a friend of Hillary's. The estate included an aviary, an in-ground pool, a large detached garage, an office bungalow, and several guest houses under renovation. The main living area was split between two buildings. The first structure contained a family room, a professional-grade kitchen, a full-size bar, and a dining room. This was called the pool house because of its proximity to the swimming pool. The second building, which was across the grounds and down a hill, was where the main sleeping quarters were. As upscale as all this may sound, the entire property had a strange hippie/swinger vibe that contrasted with its otherwise normal décor. I could feel the previous owner was a really sleazy guy who frequently threw wild parties. What's more, I discerned psychically — and it was later confirmed — that the estate had been used to film not one, but many, adult films.

After psychically surveying most of the property, I entered the sleeping quarters through sliding-glass doors off the master bedroom. I could sense something was not right. I felt compelled to get to the interior of the building. Without giving the bedroom so much as a glance, I walked straight through it onto a landing that overlooked a handsome den with a gorgeous rustic stone fireplace. It was there I froze in my tracks like a hunter stumbling across his prey. I could not believe what I was seeing. There on the floor, frolicking in front of the fireplace, were the translucent nude figures of two women and one man. The women were fair-skinned and young. One had blonde hair and the other light brown. The man was very slim, modestly athletic, and had a lean hollow face, pronounced cheek bones, short dark hair, and a beard.

I stood absolutely still. I was waiting to see if what I was seeing would vanish — as it would if I were simply imagining things. I have never seen anything like that scene, before or since. What was most amazing was the fact that the three reacted to me, as if startled by *my* presence. One of the women, who was crouching when I walked into the room, stood up quickly, letting out an inaudible gasp. In fact, both women made moves as if to cover themselves. The man seemed to glare at me, despite appearing startled at first. This whole encounter lasted less than twenty seconds before my focus softened and the vision was lost. It is one of the most incredible things I have ever experienced.

Later that evening, I sat down with Richard, a research associate, the family friend who was living with Hillary, and Hillary herself for a post-investigation cup of tea. It was only then I discovered that, despite having been called to Hillary's home because of typical haunting activity, the real problem was far worse. Hillary believed she was being molested by a "demon" while she slept.

Hillary initially refused to give any specific details as to the nature of her attacks. She only said that they were nonconsensual. We, of course, assumed this meant she was attacked physically, similarly to our client Robert whom I told you about several chapters ago. After Richard and I had earned Hillary's trust, she confided her assaults occurred only in her dreams.

At the beginning of the ordeal, Hillary said she actually looked forward to going to bed every night, where she'd participate in a kind of ongoing romance that took place in her dreams. Not long after she gave herself over to these dreams, however, they rapidly became more and more sexually explicit. Without warning, they morphed into degrading pornographic events that resulted in a demeaning loss of control. She also complained of strange physical abrasions we could not authenticate.

What Hillary described was nothing I was not already familiar with. Metaphysically speaking, the theory goes that discarnate diabolical influence begins with a kind of ongoing seduction, where an "entity" gains your trust while encouraging you to acquiesce to its presence. This process can take days, months, or even years. Once an energetic link is made, it is then assumed the "demon" persuades you to unwittingly submit to its will by fulfilling your secret needs and desires. Was this Hillary's problem?

According to Hillary, after weeks of orgasmic dreams that she both craved and deemed inappropriate, things were spinning out of control. She could no longer sleep at night because whenever she closed her eyes she could feel the "man" around her, trying to force her to do things she said she did not enjoy. Consequently, restless nights were leaving her fatigued, forcing her to take sporadic naps during the day. Before long the man began appearing in her daytime dreams as well. Now Hillary was barely getting any sleep, effectively staying up for days at a time without a full night's rest. You can imagine how weary and desperate for answers she was.

Up to that point, the only person I had shared my psychic observations with was Richard. In fact, the only person I had spoken to about the case was Richard. So I decided to subtly interrogate Hillary myself. I asked her to recap her complaint for me, challenging her to be very specific about her dreams. I wanted to hear how she understood and communicated her experiences. While Hillary spoke I listened quietly, carefully looking for inconsistencies, any clue she was exaggerating or, worse, lying about her troubles. Everything she said superficially fit Richard's version of her story, but superficial was not good enough. The devil would be in the details, I surmised. So I pressed Hillary for more. It was then she reported that, night after night, she endured visceral sexual dreams consisting of vulgar, emotionless sex where she was forced to perform unnatural acts with two females and a skinny man with a dark beard.

I nearly choked on my tea.

As I reached for a napkin, Richard tilted his head to the side and raised his eyebrow at me in a silent warning. Dismissing his gesture, I began to ask a series of increasingly personal questions related to how Hillary felt about her life in general.

Richard did not like when I asked too many personal questions. This is where he and I differed in our investigative approach. I always felt the purpose of visiting a paranormal complainant was to offer assistance. This required, in my estimation, full understanding of clients and their needs. As a strict researcher, Richard's position was we were there only to collect data. I believe both research and resolution are possible yet best achieved through understanding the totality of the situation. So, I continued my questioning and ignored Richard's pantomimed warning.

I discovered that Hillary was in her early fifties. Although recently separated, she had been married for twenty-five years. She reported a very traditional love life with no repressed urges or shame-inducing experiences in her past. She was extremely fit and attractive. She had an active social life and looked far younger than her fifty-three years. This was not a woman starved for companionship or affection. She had more than enough suitors volunteering their time. Given her candor and her friend's corroboration of her generally happy, upbeat demeanor, I had no reason to doubt anything Hillary said.

I pressed on with my questions, held my cup of tea close to my lips, and stared through the steam as Hillary continued confessing her dreams to me. When she again mentioned the two women and the skinny, bearded man I glanced sideways at Richard, who was now looking at me with increased concern.

Later that evening, Richard and I had a healthy debate as to what could have been going on at this mysterious compound. One theory we floated was that when Hillary's brain waves changed during sleep, they somehow synchronized with the environment. Perhaps this caused her to internalize the raw, amoral activities that were impressed as a "place-memory" on the holographic fabric of that particular environment. Perhaps her subconscious was reacting to the environmentally stored sexcapades in the same way we might incorporate a TV show into our dreams if we fell asleep with the television on. Could it have been that Hillary was pulling historical elements from the past into her subconscious in order to satisfy a need for affection due to the loss of her husband?

To avoid frightening Hillary into believing her dreams included real invisible beings attacking her as she slept, I decided not to tell her about my psychic visions. I remain convinced this was the correct thing to do. Given the fact Hillary's paranormal dilemma ceased once the stress of her divorced passed, I am confident this decision was correct.

There is no way to know for certain what happened to Hillary. What is apparent, however, is the experiences at Hillary's compound demonstrate a clear exchange of information between consciousness and the environment. From a ghost hunter's perspective, the uncanny similarity between my clairvoyant vision and Hillary's dreams created more questions than answers. Said queries do not call into question nor confirm the reality of ghosts in my opinion. I believe my psychic sensitivity simply allowed my mind to animate the information stored in the environment much the same as Hillary's did while she slept. Agree or disagree, the commonality in our perceptions is compelling. I do not think we can deny in this instance that there was interplay between Hillary's mind and the environment, but exactly what this interplay was, I honestly cannot say for certain.

By now you have a basic understanding of how extrasensory information can be seen within the mind's eye. But how does this explain the psychic ability to see invisible things outside of your head as if they were separate from you?

Some people speculate that clairvoyance functions just like conventional eyesight, meaning certain people can look out at the world and see things that, somehow, the rest of us cannot see. Even as someone

THE RATIONAL PSYCHIC

who has had this experience, I believe it's completely reasonable to assume any person who says they see invisible things might be crazy, lying, or seriously kidding themselves. When all chance for fraud is ruled out, when the visions a supposed psychic reports turn out to be true, then it's hard to dismiss the claim that sometimes, for some people, it's possible to see the invisible outside of the mind.

Clairvoyance falls into two categories. When you see information within your mind's eye it is called *subjective clairvoyance.* When you see information outside of your mind, as if it were in the physical environment, it is called *objective clairvoyance.* The common-sense explanation for objective clairvoyance is that since animals like cats, dogs, and even insects can hear sounds or see light far below or beyond the range of human perception, perhaps certain psychic people have some unusual biological adaption that allows them to do this, too. But since extrasensory perception is an adaptation of the mind — a function of consciousness — and human beings are not physically equipped to see the ultraviolet spectrum like an insect or hear high-pitched frequencies like a dog, so I do not think comparing a psychic person to a less evolved animal is a logical way to explain objective clairvoyance.

When it comes to clairvoyance, it often seems that people who claim to see information outside their minds are somehow more psychic or superhuman than the rest of us. The truth of the matter is that clairvoyance has little or nothing to do with physical "superhuman" seeing or sensing abilities. The difference between objective and subjective clairvoyance may seem important, but in reality it is negligible. Whether psychic information is perceived internally in the third eye or seen externally in the environment, it is really only our judgment about how the information is displayed that makes objective perception seem more fantastic. This is because, despite where and how they appear, all clairvoyant images blossom from within your mind.

Think of your mind as a movie projector. And then imagine that extrasensory energy encoded with information is the film that feeds into your subconscious. If your brain has the correct frame of reference on file, you will be able to decipher this energetic film using the light of your conscious awareness to animate and focus this information into discernible mental images. Whether your mind plays back this information subjectively in your mind's eye or projects it simply depends on the depth of your relaxation during clairvoyant service. If the psychic images seen in the environment — like the ghost people by the fire at Hillary's — and those viewed in your mind's eye are both inner products of your consciousness, one question remains: how does the human mind project extrasensory information, making it seem like you are seeing invisible images, separate from you, in the actual physical environment?

Closed-Eye Visualizations

Some psychics — including myself — report seeing invisible people, scenes from the past and future, and even objects or events superimposed over or within their immediate physical surroundings. It's understandably a hard pill to swallow. I mean seriously, I'm seeing something that is invisible? How can this be so? One possible explanation comes from a psychological phenomenon called *closed-eye visualizations.*

Closed-eye visualizations (CEVs) are considered a distinct class of hallucinations that can be induced chemically or through deeply relaxing meditative exercises. When you shut your eyes and focus on your third eye, you might see abstract light, color, and movement — otherwise known as CEVs. CEVs can occur either with your eyes shut or in a darkened room. Although I agree with some academics who claim CEVs are often meaningless flashes of light, writing them off entirely feels premature. Although CEVs are a normal biological process, it has been my experience that they can be precursors to verifiable clairvoyance.

The key is to distinguish normal biological events from the extraordinary nature of genuine extrasensory perception. Without proper understanding of both mind and body, psychic aspirants can easily fall victim to old wives' tales and the clever marketing of new-age commercial mysticism. Remember when I told you of the "expert" who claimed you can see angels by noticing lights out of the corners of your eyes? By now you know twinkles of light do not indicate the presence of any discarnate intelligence. The luminous sparks people see both with their eyes closed and out of the corners of their eyes are actually a particular type of CEV called a *phosphene*. Phosphenes are nothing more than biochemically created flashes of light produced from within the eye. They are not caused by any kind of magical, mystical, or divine entity.

When I first attempted clairvoyance, I experienced closed-eye visualizations exactly as science and reason dictate I should. First I saw darkness, which then evolved into an ever-shifting, gritty gray cloud. It looked very much like cigarette ash swirling in water. Different colored luminous sparks occasionally twinkled off and on. All of this drifted in and out of focus until my mind's eye morphed into a kind of strange kaleidoscope, where fragments of shapes flowed in and out of my field of vision. Then objects, people, and places came into focus before dissolving back into the watery ash.

What I eventually learned by observing my closed-eye visualizations is that the images that can appear among the mental noise are not always random or meaningless. Now, whether I am sitting with a client, offering remote assistance on a missing person's case, or identifying the history of a particular location, I do pay attention to the kaleidoscope of my mind. Like a piece of Polaroid film, I can expect a verifiable image to appear.

There are five levels of perception associated with closed-eye visualizations. The first is when you close your eyes and only see meaningless noise in the visual field — blackness and/or random light and dark regions with no distinct shape or order. The second level of CEV consists of passing light and dark shadows and possibly flashes of color. The third level consists of patterns, motion, and color. This stage is sometimes associated with deep concentration and hypnagogic hallucinations (the visions one sees when drifting off to sleep, in between wakefulness and deep sleep).

Once we enter the fourth level of closed-eye visualization we are in a deeply relaxed state. This is where we find a rational explanation for objective clairvoyance. During level-4 CEV, the grainy clouds and flashes of light in the visual field disappear over the horizon like a passing storm, leaving you in total darkness. Your mind might become virtually still, uninterrupted by normal thinking, sound, or vision. You may also feel like you are moving. The most important aspect of a level-4 CEV is that, if you open your eyes, you may see the contents of your mind projected outward, superimposed on your field of vision. At this level, you may have the ability to see your clairvoyant image projected as if it were within the environment.

But wait, I said there were five levels of closed-eye visualization. Level 5 is where a person risks being diagnosed as insane. At this stage, your self-generated internal perceptions override your physical sense perceptions, causing you to confuse reality with fantasy. A psychic who is mentally and emotionally healthy will never reach this dissociative point. As I've said before, responsible practitioners always remain emotionally detached from — and require objective verification for — their psychic perceptions.

The Mentalist

Not too long ago, I was hired to participate in a special-features documentary for the DVD release of the hit CBS television show *The Mentalist*. The program is about a former TV psychic who helps police solve crimes. The special documentary for the DVD includes an interesting cast of former law-enforcement officers, skeptics, and scientists all specially chosen to offer their opinion on psychics and their role in solving crimes, as *The Mentalist's* fictitious lead character does. I was selected as the psychic expert, the real-life "mentalist" as it were.

I arrived at the production office in Studio City, California, delighted to meet the creative team behind the documentary. It was a small group, just a sound man, a lighting guy, and the project's supervising producer acting as interviewer. The plan was to interview each expert individually, and then edit all the commentary into one conversation.

For a little over an hour I sat in front of a green screen fielding questions on a broad range of psychic topics. I explained what it is like to be psychic, how one might work in conjunction with law enforcement, and I shared some of my personal experiences consulting on missing persons cases. All the while, I compared my life to the characters and events that appeared each week on the show. It was a great discussion overall, but toward the end I noticed that the questions, while respectful, were getting increasingly cynical. I had a sense the producer was getting fed up with suppressing his disbelief about what I do. Perhaps he felt I was insulting his intelligence. I didn't know for sure. All I knew was that I wanted to answer his questions and get back to the office because I had clients scheduled later that afternoon.

As the interview was winding down, my feelings were verified. I was in the middle of explaining psychometry when the producer cut me off midsentence from behind the camera. "So you're saying that you can learn things about a person just by holding an object that belongs to them?"

"Yes, that's right," I said. I went on to explain that, typically, psychometry works best when using a metallic object such as keys or jewelry. I went on to give an example of the kinds of information one might learn by applying psychometry. Clearly not listening, the producer pulled a gold ring off his finger and tossed it at me while I was still answering his question.

"Tell me what you get from this," he interrupted.

I had a flashback of playing hot potato as a little boy. I've always hated being put on the spot. Moreover, in my line of work, situations like this are often "damned if you do, damned if you don't," otherwise known as lose-lose. If you refuse to prove your ability on the spot, you look like you are hiding something. If you accept the challenge out of an egotistic desire for approval or validation, more often than not your ability will fail. Even if you do succeed in demonstrating psychic ability to a cynic, there is always the chance your accuser will claim you tricked or cheated them. Like I said, lose-lose.

Psychic work is a service and should never be used as a means for personal aggrandizement. For real honest-to-goodness psychics, every demonstration is an experiment. Sometimes it works and sometimes it doesn't. After all, if researchers could successfully replicate and explain the exact mechanism of extrasensory perception without failure, it would not be called a phenomenon. Nerves, anxiety, your overall emotional well-being and even environmental influences can, and do, affect psychic cognition. Thus, challenging a psychic to prove themselves on the spot is not really a level playing field. Asking someone to prove themselves at anything is anxiety-provoking enough, but add a video camera, plus the knowledge that you'll look like you're copping out if you attempt to explain the variables that go into psychic success, and you can see how hard it would be to maintain the clear, calm mind required for a psychic demonstration.

I do not perform tricks on command like a circus monkey. So my first instinct was to return the ring and offer some kind of excuse for why I could not or would not perform on the spot. Fortunately, I was over-come by an onset of self-consciousness that caused me to retreat inward for a second. But when a sense of calm came over me, I recognized the work was really not about me. I confidently looked up and said, "It's a little distracting in here with the heat from the lights and everything. Why don't you give me a minute to center myself and we can talk in one of the empty offices down the hall." Looking a little shocked, the producer obliged.

I found my way to an empty office, stretched the tension from my muscles, cleared my mind, and after a few moments was joined by the producer, Gary. We sat down opposite each other and I asked Gary if he had any questions. He said he didn't. As matter of courtesy, I then briefly explained how a psychic reading works, just the way I would for any client beginning a session with me. After a moment of silence, I gently curled my left hand into a fist around Gary's ring, closed my eyes, and slowed my breathing to a deeply relaxed rhythmic pace.

As I opened my sensitivities an image of an old man suddenly came to mind. I shared it with Gary, who merely shrugged. I then became aware of my chest being opened for heart surgery. I could see the exposed organs and feel doctors and nurses crowding over me, as my point of view changed to that of someone lying on an operating table inside a surgical theater. I spent several minutes describing for Gary a variety of serious ailments, including that the ring-owner's kidneys were shutting down. Gary remained quiet. He acknowledged none of what I shared with him.

Seeing that the medical issues apparently had no relevance to Gary, I moved on. Besides, I did not want to stress him out if I was seeing twenty years into his future. I shifted gears and accepted information into my awareness concerning Gary's wife. I could see very clearly there was something unique about his wife's hair. "It is a joke," I said, "like a family joke about her hair being so big or bright or something. It screams at you in a way. I can't tell what it is."

I focused harder but this hair business just did not make sense to me. Gary laughed and confided his wife had very bright red hair when she was young. It then became very clear that the "I," the owner of this ring, had had a growth removed from his scalp, under his hairline. I could literally feel the incision and see the removal of a small mass from someone's head. Upon hearing my description of this, Gary gasped. He was genuinely surprised. From that moment forward, his demeanor softened. He went from skeptically tolerant to openly curious. As it turned out, Gary had indeed, very recently, had a suspicious growth excised from his scalp exactly where I had indicated.

For the next few minutes a positive flow of information allowed Gary and me to marvel at the reality of extrasensory potential. During a moment's pause while I was collecting a new impression from the psychic atmosphere, Gary confessed that the ring I was holding was actually a family heirloom. At first I felt deceived, but Gary interrupted this thought, telling me the heart surgery and subsequent maladies I had spoken of earlier were an exact match to his ailing father. He then looked at me half-amused, gauging my response.

I was confused. "Wait, the ring is not yours?" I asked.

"No. Well . . . yes . . . I mean . . ." Gary stammered. "My father wore that ring for fifty years, but now it's mine."

Things began to make sense. It was clear I was picking up on two different energies impressed upon the ring. Initially, I set aside the medical information I perceived because it seemed irrelevant to Gary. I reasoned the ailments and surgeries I saw were future events, despite the fact they felt very immediate. Now that I knew the ring once belonged to Gary's father, I refocused my attention on the original health concerns that had appeared in my mind's eye. I knew there was something important about these issues. Something Gary needed to know.

As I reinitiated our reading, just like before, my sensitivity kept zeroing in on Gary's dad's kidneys. Based on what I was being shown, I had no doubt that ultimately they would prove to be the real cause of his dad's demise. Since it is considered unethical for a psychic to predict a person's death, all I could do was try to convince Gary his dad needed to have his kidneys examined as soon as possible. No matter how many times I brought this issue up, and despite the fact that everything else I had said was on the mark, Gary resisted. What could I say? I am not a doctor. With his dad's bad heart and several other pertinent medical issues actually presenting, there really was no logical reason for Gary to take my advice.

Before long, the energy in the room subsided and we closed our session. Gary and I shook hands. I thanked him for the opportunity to participate in his documentary and we parted ways. A few months later, I received a complimentary copy of *The Mentalist* DVD with a note from Gary. He told me his father had passed, "coincidentally" due to the causes I had described during our reading. Should I have insisted

Gary mention his father's kidneys to his doctors? I do not believe so. As a psychic, all you can responsibly do is give the information you receive. Young seers often assume that perceiving information means they are personally responsible to guide others according to their vision. Over time, practical experience creates humility that erodes this youthful self-importance. Maturity brings the realization that you, as a psychic, have no spiritual authority to impose yourself on circumstances that are none of your business. When I learned Gary's father did suffer from complications with his kidneys, part of me momentarily wondered if things would have been different had I asserted myself. But perhaps the lessons of love, life, and death are far more important than extrasensory perception — or anyone who claims to wield it.

9

A NEW
HORIZON

We want to know the truth about reincarnation, we want proof of the
survival of the soul, we listen to the assertion of clairvoyants and to the
conclusions of psychical research, but we never ask, never, how to live.

JIDDU KRISHNAMURTI

It was one of those days. I had been on the go since five-thirty in the
morning, and somehow I had forgotten to eat. After a long, uncomfortable flight and an even longer car ride, I arrived at my hotel well after dark,
completely starving. I had a late dinner and passed out in my room. Three
hours later, I woke up starving again, as if I had not eaten for days. (Jet
lag strikes again.) Unfortunately, the hotel had no late-night food service
and when I looked out the window all I could see was ice, snow, and the
lights of a single-lane road cutting into frozen blackness. There were no
restaurants or convenience stores for miles. I had to eat something or else
I knew I was going to spend the rest of the night wide awake.

With some effort I found a vending machine on the floor above
mine. After convincing the front desk clerk to change a five dollar bill
into twenty quarters, I nearly poisoned myself on a buffet of Pop-Tarts,
pretzels, and some kind of manufactured "home style" cookie. In my

right mind I would never ever eat like this, but I really felt like I was starving. Tomorrow would be my first day filming a pilot for a paranormal television series. I had to be rested. Junk food or not, I ate like it was my last meal.

In the morning, after an amazing breakfast, I knelt on the center of my bed for my morning meditation. Within minutes I was perfectly still in both mind and body. Each inhalation of breath flowed through my nasal passages like a soft breeze. I do not know how long I was in the zone, but after a while I refocused my awareness on the stillness of my mind and asked to see any pertinent information concerning that day's filming location.

Mental pictures slowly drifted before my mind's eye while subtle, feeling-based impressions filled my awareness. Clairvoyantly, I perceived several unidentified bodies buried in the ground. I knew the bodies were connected to the supposedly haunted house we would be filming in that day. There were images of cats, something about some kind of nursemaid or servant, and a lot of other sordid visions having to do with the basement of the house. I sat in my psychic awareness for a few more minutes, taking mental notes, until I causally glanced at the alarm clock next to the bed. A car was scheduled to pick me up in about half an hour. I needed to complete my meditation and get ready.

When I exited the solitude of inner stillness, my logical mind quickly began picking apart my clairvoyance. A hidden graveyard? Really? That was just too hokey. Am I really going to show up on set and tell the owner of the home there are bodies under his property? That just seemed way too "Hollywood haunted house" to be accurate. This was the kind of thing every half-wit psychic says when examining a reportedly haunted house. Was I really going to say on camera that the house was haunted because there were dead bodies buried on the property? It was such a cliché. I would look like a buffoon. No matter what my logical mind said, my gut was telling me there were indeed bodies under the ground where I was going to be filming later that day.

I got off the bed and walked toward the bathroom, still thinking about what might happen if I told the TV crew there were human bodies under the house. What if I tell them and I am wrong? I didn't necessarily care about being wrong per se; even the best of us make mistakes. It was just that it seemed so outrageous to claim there is a conveniently forgotten or somehow unknown graveyard associated with this allegedly haunted house. Besides, I am known for being much more rational than saying something so seemingly crazy. What was I going to do?

As I shaved and brushed my teeth, my mind continued critiquing what I saw during my mediation. It was now clear that not only were there bodies in the ground, but there was a tunnel too — a secret underground tunnel that connected the "haunted house" with the homes next door. Oh boy, I thought, this just keeps getting better. Where is this information coming from? Maybe I would play it safe and just keep all of this information to myself. Yet no matter how I tried to dismiss what I was sensing, I knew the tunnel and graves were real — no matter how hokey this seemed.

I decided that after I arrived on location I would take a walk by myself to see if I could find any sign of a graveyard. Before I did this, however, I would tell my cohost and one of the producers about my impressions. That way, they could corroborate my prediction if there were indeed graves on the property. If I could find no proof of what I saw in my mind's eye, then I would say nothing to the director — and nothing while I was on camera. This sounded like a good plan — too bad I did not stick to it.

By the time I finished getting dressed, an SUV was already waiting downstairs to take me to the set. I hurried down, climbed in, and said good morning to the driver, my cohost, and a producer from the production company. We had about a forty-minute commute, which was nice as it gave us ample time to get acquainted. During our drive we talked about where we were from, as well as how our flights had been.

Once the introductions were out of the way, I nonchalantly inquired about the graves. No one except the producer had actually been to the set, so when I asked the question the banter in the car came to an end. I noticed the producer trying to be diplomatic before she answered very politely that there were no signs of any graves at the house. I downplayed my disappointment and discreetly changed the subject before revisiting the topic one more time a few minutes later. Again, the producer asserted that there were no graves on or near the property we were filming that day.

The location where we were shooting was an amazing pre-Victorian house built in 1811 overlooking the Hudson River. It was situated alongside a row of equally impressive homes from the same time period. When we arrived, we turned onto a side street and parked just opposite the back door. My colleagues were anxious to get out of the cold so they darted indoors. For my part, I froze. It was not that I was cold — I was completely crestfallen. From where I was standing I could see the entire backyard, all four hundred square feet of it. Clearly, if there were any graves here, somebody would know.

My logical left brain stepped in to comfort me. I reassured myself that I had dodged a bullet. If I would just stick to the plan and keep my mouth shut about the bodies, I'd avoid humiliation over all this nonsense. Tiny yard or not, something still did not feel right. The sense of death was even more potent to me now, despite what I could see with my eyes. Like a moth to a flame, I slowly drifted into the backyard. I was unsure what exactly I was looking for, but I was compelled to search for any sign of a grave. I found nothing. All I uncovered was the distinct sense that the property used to be much, much larger. Oh well, I thought, I'd better get inside.

Once inside, I discovered a typical film set. There were lots of camera bags, laptops, light set-ups, and people darting back and forth focused on accomplishing their various assigned tasks in order to keep the shoot on schedule and under budget. Someone very kindly offered me a cup of tea, and the next thing I knew a producer was introducing me to the executive in charge. We exchanged some polite conversation and discussed what we were going to film that day when . . . it just popped out of my mouth: "You know there's a tunnel under this property right?"

The executive's mouth fell open. I had taken him completely by surprise. "What did you say?" he asked.

"A tunnel. There's a tunnel under this house that connects it to the houses next door. Does the owner know? It might be cool to shoot."

Before I could elaborate, the executive politely asked me to hold on one second. He called the owner of the home over and asked him to repeat something he had confided a half-hour before my arrival. Yes, you guessed it. There was indeed a tunnel under the house.

Later that morning, I asked the owner of the home about the graves connected to the house. He said there were no graves.

"Are you sure?" I inquired. "The graves could be as far as about a hundred yards from the house, maybe less, maybe more, but roughly within one hundred or so yards from where we are standing."

The homeowner shook his head. He had no idea what I was talking about. I must have sounded crazy. After all, the man would know whether he's living over a graveyard right? While I could find no proof of the graves I was seeing in my mind's eye, my conversation with the homeowner was not completely fruitless. He did reveal that once upon a time, the area behind the house had been farmland belonging to the original homeowner. Could there be a graveyard where there are now streets and buildings, I wondered?

Despite the earlier warnings from my logical mind, I could not help but yammer on — while the cameras were rolling — about the bodies connected to the house. Then it struck me. Something was not right about what I was intuiting. I could now see bodies lying askew. The corpses were not boxed and interred in an orderly manner. There were no headstones. This was definitely not an official graveyard I was seeing. It was a special, private burial place that was absolutely meant only for the privileged people who had lived along the riverfront. Like a flash of lightning, another important piece of information hit me. I realized that although there were no individual headstones, there *was* a grave marker. I could see it as clear as a bell! If we could just find that marker we would find the bodies. This I now knew for sure. Sadly, when I asked the property owner about the grave marker, he just shook his head politely dismissing my vision. He still had no idea what I was talking about.

Later that day, as the winter sun dipped below the horizon and production began to wind down, I decided to take a walk. Maybe if I could find a graveyard that dated back to the mid-1800s in the neighborhood behind the house where the farm used to be, this would help solve the mystery of the invisible burial site that I kept seeing again and again. I grabbed my coat and headed out. Forty minutes later, chilled and a bit discouraged, I returned empty-handed. I had finally resigned myself to the fact that my vision of a ghoulish mass-burial site was either wrong or impossible to confirm.

Oh well, I sighed to myself as I climbed back into the SUV for the ride back to the hotel. It had nevertheless been a very good day. I had made some great new friends and I was feeling happy and very fortunate to be doing what I love.

The next morning, the homeowner picked my cohost and me up to take us to that day's film location. This was a bit unusual, but since he was also scheduled to participate in that day's shooting and had to pass by our hotel anyway, the production company agreed to have him transport us. I climbed into the back seat of the car with a cup of hot mint tea in my hand, said good morning, and before long we were zooming down the freeway. We enjoyed teasing each other a bit while recollecting humorous moments from our first day filming together. Then the conversation turned serious.

"So," the homeowner said to me, catching my eye in his rearview mirror, "remember those graves you were telling me about?"

"Yes," I replied, trying to conceal my excitement.

"Well, I remembered last night what you were talking about," he said. From his bag, he withdrew a page printed off the Internet and passed it over the seat to me.

I was holding the answer to my clairvoyant mystery. Under a banner that read *The New York Times,* 1906, was the story of an unnatural disaster caused by the shady business dealings of the home's original owner. Despite my self-doubt over my cliché visions, it turned out the former owner of the supposedly haunted house was directly responsible for a landslide that consumed twenty nearby residences and their nineteen innocent occupants when, as mayor of the town, he allowed a brick manufacturer to excavate clay too close to local homes. Profit had been put ahead of people. The improper digging resulted in five city streets collapsing down a hillside. The carnage and resulting fires were so horrible that many victims were never recovered from beneath the earth and debris.

My psychic visions were all making sense now. The *New York Times* article validated everything I had perceived about the house, including the sense of a disheveled mass grave, the impression that only people who lived along the riverfront were in the burial site, and even its rough location. Later that afternoon, I was privileged to visit the disaster site. All that was left of where those beautiful homes once stood was a 150-foot cliff—and a simple commemorative plaque overlooking the Hudson River. It was awful to think that these people had died so needlessly because of greed. I offered a silent prayer for those entombed under the snow-encrusted earth, as the sun retreated under what seemed a new horizon.

While watching the sun go down I unexpectedly felt a sense of closure that affected me very deeply. It occurred to me that it is not what happens after death that matters, it is how we live that counts. Sometimes my analytical mind still wants to reason that my empathetic near-death experience at the time of my sister's death was just a coincidence—a result, perhaps, of sleep paralysis or some sort of hypnagogic hallucination. But the emotional effect of that precognitive ENDE was so profound; I cannot intellectually dismiss it without feeling as if I am betraying a precious gift.

My ENDE taught me unequivocally that regardless of what you believe, you are so much more than what you can see. Perhaps whether or not something is objectively real is not really the point when it comes to the paranormal. Maybe the lesson here is to view all perceptions, paranormal or otherwise, as wonderful tools that can help you discover, heal, and live as your authentic self.

Standing alone that day looking out over the Hudson River, I was reminded of a passage from Edgar Cayce's *Search for God:*

> When we are asked the question "Do you know yourself?" why is
> it that we cannot say "Yes"? Within each of us there are certainly
> great storehouses of abilities and capacities which we have
> never used. If they were manifested, we would see ourselves in a
> different light. We would understand the real functions of our
> physical bodies in relation to our mental and spiritual bodies.
> Until we are better acquainted with ourselves, we are barriers in
> the way of our own development.[1]

Paranormal perceptions can haunt you if you choose to deny responsibility for your life. But they can *heal* you if you choose to embrace the spiritual work necessary to resolve the issues your mind projects into the world. The choice is yours.

My wish for you is that you use what you have learned here to challenge the fear-based metaphors and mystical assumptions that compel less-informed people to passively respond to their existence, rather than create it. As a sensitive person you must remember that what you sense and how you feel always teaches you the quality of *your* consciousness, whether you are looking into the eyes of someone who loves you or sensing things that go bump in the night. Armed with this awareness — and a willingness to own who and what you are — you can make powerful choices concerning who you wish to be and what you want to experience.

Indeed, my paranormal pursuits have led me to a new spiritual understanding of my relationship with the world around me and the people in it. I am grateful for my psychic talents, but without love, without caring for others, and a without a deeper appreciation for ourselves and our relationships, psychic ability is meaningless and life is meaningless. Your spiritual value and sense of purpose has nothing to do with anything psychic. I am utterly convinced of this. Pursuing psychic development in place of spiritual development is nothing but escapism. To evolve we must commit to owning who we are, not as extrasensory people but simply as perfectly flawed human beings.

These were my thoughts as I watched the sun set over the Hudson River that wintry evening. Finally at peace with myself, as the icy winds whipped off the river, stinging my face, I began to reflect on my life.

Looking back at who I was so many, many years ago — beginning the day my sister died — I am now grateful for how pained, frustrated, and angry I sometimes was when searching for meaning and answers to my questions about the paranormal. Those tough times forced me to realize there is a world out there that is far more important than anything paranormal, including my need to understand my abilities. Recalling the liberation my disabled sister felt after being released from her body is all it took to remind me what is really important. Thus, I have given up looking for *reasons* to believe in extrasensory perception. Instead, I believe in you, I believe in me, and I believe in love.

NOTES

Introduction

1. Bootie Cosgrove-Mather, "Poll: Most Believe in Psychic Phenomena," CBS News, February 11, 2009, cbsnews.com/2100 -500160_162-507515.htm

2. Bruce Bower, "Visions For All," *Science News*. April 7, 2012, 23.

Chapter 2 Laying the Foundation

1. Andrew Nichols, *Ghost Detective: Adventures of a Parapsychologist* (Bloomington, IN: Authorhouse, 2004), 201.

2. Ibid.

Chapter 3 Psi, Psychosis, and Psychic Development

1. Richard S. Broughton, *Parapsychology: The Controversial Science* (New York: Ballantine Books, 1992), 25.

Chapter 4 Dissecting Paranormal Evil

1. Diamond is quoted in: John Bradshaw, *Healing the Shame That Binds You,* rev. ed. (Deerfield Beach, FL: Health Communications, Inc., 2005), 4.

2. Ibid.

3. Michael Gazzaniga and Joseph LeDoux, *The Integrated Mind* (New York: Plenum Press, 1978)

4. Malachi Martin, *Hostage to the Devil: The Possession and Exorcism of Five Contemporary Americans* (New York: Harper One, 1992), xx.

5. Annie Besant and C. W. Leadbeater, *Thought Forms* (Wheaton, IL: Theosophical Publishing House, 1999), 16.

6. Lena Barnes Jefts, *The Questionnaire for the Teacher and the Investigator: One Hundred Questions and Answers on the Philosophy of Spiritualism* (Lily Dale, NY: Summit Publications), II, 2; I, 20.

7. Jack Kornfield, *A Lamp in the Darkness: Illuminating the Path Through Difficult Times* (Boulder, CO: Sounds True, 2011), 4–5.

Chapter 5 Redefining Reality

1. Leo Talamonti, *Forbidden Universe: Mysteries of the Psychic World* (New York: Stein and Day, 1974), 44.

2. Khei, *A Brief Course in Mediumship: Rosicrucian Viewpoint on Intercommunication between the Physical and Spiritual Worlds* (Kessinger Publishing Company, 1996), 29.

3. Ibid.

4. Ibid.

5. Andrew Newberg, Eugene D'Aquili, and Vince Rause, *Why God Won't Go Away: Brain Science and the Biology of Belief* (New York: Ballantine Book, Random House Publishing Group, 2001), 25.

6. Ibid.

7. Simeon Hein, "How Remote Viewing Works, Part 3" (lecture, The International UFO Conference, 2005), accessed March 27, 2012, www.youtube.com/watch?feature=endscreen&v=xs-X1Ria8BU&NR=1

8. Michael Talbot, *The Holographic Universe* (New York: Harper Collins, 1991), 164.

9. Ibid.

10. Ervin Laszlo, "Cosmic Symphony — A Deeper Look at Quantum Consciousness," April 9, 2010, ervinlaszlo.com

/notebook/2010/04/09/cosmic-symphony-a-deeper-look-at
-quantum-consciousness-2/.

11. Lynne McTaggart, *The Field: The Quest for the Secret Force of the Universe* (New York: Harper Collins, 2008), 95.

12. Ibid.

13. Gen. 1:2 (AV)

14. "'Perfect' liquid hot enough to be quark soup," *Science News.* Febrary 15, 2010.

15. Talbot, *The Holographic Universe,* 54.

16. Deepak Chopra, *How to Know God: The Soul's Journey into the Mystery of Mysteries* (New York: Three Rivers Press, 2000), 265.

17. Edgar Mitchell, *The Quantum Hologram and ESP* (UFO TV Studios, 2005), DVD.

18. Jim Al-Khalili, *Atom: The Illusion of Reality* (BBC4), accessed March 27, 2012, video.google.com/videoplay?do cid=-1406370011028154810

19. Dean Radin, *Entangled Minds: Extrasensory Experiences in a Quantum Reality* (New York: Pocket Books, 2006), 137.

20. Ervin Laszlo, *Science and the Akashic Field: An Integral Theory of Everything* (Rochester, VT: Inner Traditions, 2004), 80.

21. Ibid., 81.

Chapter 6 Anatomy of a Psychic

1. Daniel Goleman, *Social Intelligence: The New Science of Human Relationships* (New York: Bantam Books, 2006), 42.

2. Wayne Muller, *Legacy of the Heart: The Spiritual Advantages of a Painful Childhood* (New York: Fireside, 1992), xiii.

3. Gary E. Schwartz, *The Truth about Medium: Extraordinary Experiments with the Real Allison DuBois of NBC's* Medium *and other Remarkable Psychics* (Charlottesville, VA: Hampton Roads, 2005), 25.

4. Ibid.

5. Paul T. Mason and Randi Kreger, *Stop Walking on Eggshells: Taking Your Life Back When Someone You Care About Has*

Borderline Personality Disorder (Oakland, CA: New Harbinger Publications, 1998), 44.

6. Ibid.

7. David Richo, *When the Past Is Present: Healing the Emotional Wounds that Sabotage our Relationships* (Boston: Shambhala Publications, 2008), 124.

8. Ibid.

9. Joseph McMoneagle, *Remote Viewing Secrets: A Handbook* (Charlottesville, VA: Hampton Roads, 2000), 40.

10. Ibid., 41.

11. Julie Levin, "Somatic Awareness and Empathic Resonance in Psychotherapy" *East Bay Therapist,* November/December 2005.

12. Ibid.

13. Tara Bennett-Goleman, *Emotional Alchemy: How the Mind Can Heal the Heart* (New York: Harmony Books, 2001), 144.

14. Ibid.

15. Radin, *Entangled Minds,* 164–168.

Chapter 7 Emotions and Psychic Ability

1. Bennett-Goleman, *Emotional Alchemy,* 178.

2. Edward A. Charlesworth, *Psi and the Imaginary Dream: Including an Exploration with Monozygotic and Dizygotic Twins and Autogenic Training* (Houston TX: University of Houston, 1974), 85.

3. Daniel Goleman, *Destructive Emotions: A Scientific Dialogue with the Dalai Lama* (New York: Bantam Dell, 2003), 203.

Chapter 8 Seeing the Invisible

1. Chopra, *How to Know God,* 6.

2. Ibid., 16.

3. Ibid.

4. Rick Strassman, *DMT: The Spirit Molecule: A Doctor's Revolutionary Research into the Biology of Near-Death and Mystical Experiences* (Rochester, VT: Park Street Press, 2001), 42.

5. Ibid.

6. Talbot, *The Holographic Universe,* 68.

Chapter 9 A New Horizon

1. Edgar Cayce, *Search for God, Book* 1 (Virginia Beach, VA: Association for Research and Enlightenment, Inc., 1970), 33.

INDEX

ABOUT THE AUTHOR

Jack Rourke is a practicing psychic, media consultant, and parapsychological researcher who developed his Rational Psychic approach over the last fifteen years in response to clients who believed they were paranormally afflicted. By aligning his work with the sciences of psychology, physics, and Eastern philosophy, Jack emphasizes personal accountability, embodiment, self awareness, and self-love as pathways to authentic spiritual awakening.

For more information about Jack Rourke's workshops, speaking engagements, or media appearances, please friend him on Facebook, follow him on Twitter, or visit jackrourke.net.

ABOUT SOUNDS TRUE

Sounds True is a multimedia publisher whose mission is to inspire and support personal transformation and spiritual awakening. Founded in 1985 and located in Boulder, Colorado, we work with many of the leading spiritual teachers, thinkers, healers, and visionary artists of our time. We strive with every title to preserve the essential "living wisdom" of the author or artist. It is our goal to create products that not only provide information to a reader or listener, but that also embody the quality of a wisdom transmission.

For those seeking genuine transformation, Sounds True is your trusted partner. At SoundsTrue.com you will find a wealth of free resources to support your journey, including exclusive weekly audio interviews, free downloads, interactive learning tools, and other special savings on all our titles.

To listen to a podcast interview with Sounds True publisher Tami Simon and author Jack Rourke, please visit SoundsTrue.com/bonus/RationalPsychic.